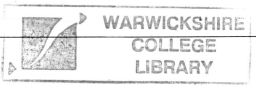

DK EYEWITNESS GUIDES

BUTTERFLY
& MOTH

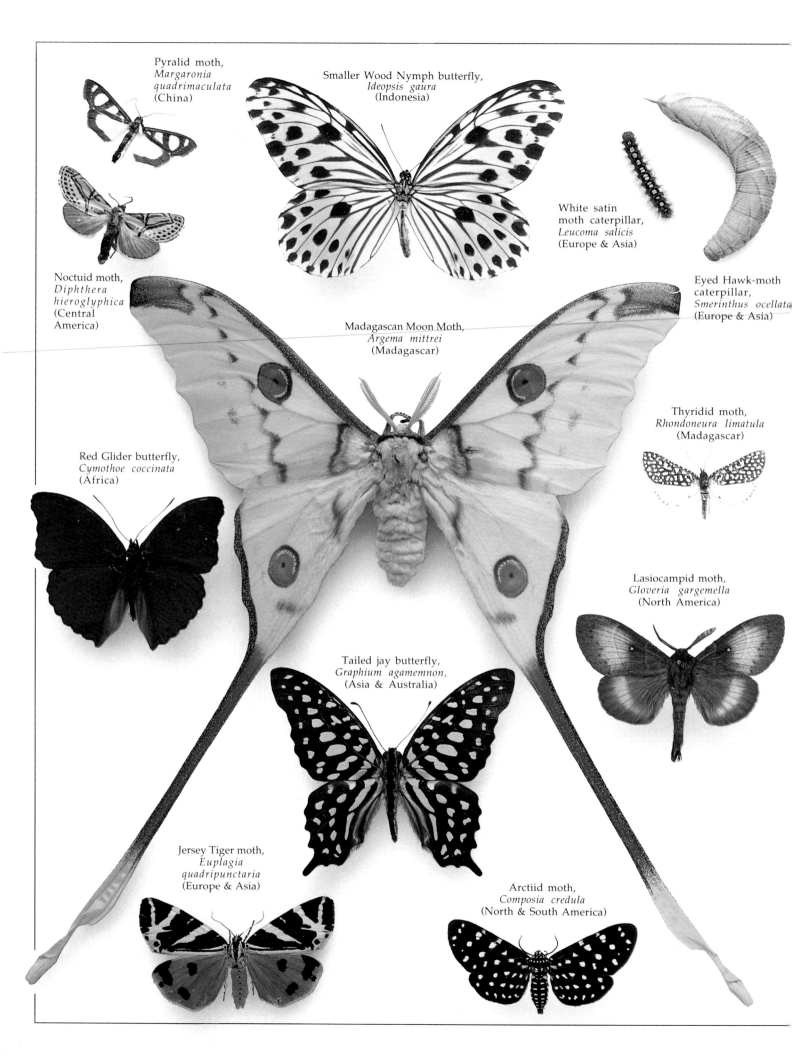

Pyralid moth,
*Margaronia
quadrimaculata*
(China)

Smaller Wood Nymph butterfly,
Ideopsis gaura
(Indonesia)

White satin
moth caterpillar,
Leucoma salicis
(Europe & Asia)

Noctuid moth,
*Diphthera
hieroglyphica*
(Central
America)

Madagascan Moon Moth,
Argema mittrei
(Madagascar)

Eyed Hawk-moth
caterpillar,
Smerinthus ocellata
(Europe & Asia)

Thyridid moth,
Rhondoneura limatula
(Madagascar)

Red Glider butterfly,
Cymothoe coccinata
(Africa)

Lasiocampid moth,
Gloveria gargemella
(North America)

Tailed jay butterfly,
Graphium agamemnon,
(Asia & Australia)

Jersey Tiger moth,
*Euplagia
quadripunctaria*
(Europe & Asia)

Arctiid moth,
Composia credula
(North & South America)

Noctuid moth,
Mazuca strigitincta
(Africa)

Noctuid moth,
Apsarasa radians
(India & Indonesia)

DK EYEWITNESS GUIDES

BUTTERFLY & MOTH

Written by
PAUL WHALLEY

Tiger Pierid
butterfly,
*Dismorphia
amphione*
(Central &
South America)

Birdwing butterfly,
Troides hypolitus,
(Indonesia)

Noctuid moth,
Baorisa hieroglyphica
(India & Southeast
Asia)

Kentish Glory moth,
Endromis versicolora
(Europe)

Hairstreak butterfly,
Thecla coronata
(South America)

DK

DORLING KINDERSLEY
London • New York • Sydney • Moscow
www.dk.com
in association with
THE NATURAL HISTORY
MUSEUM LONDON

Peacock butterfly,
Inachis io
(Europe & Asia)

DK

A DORLING KINDERSLEY BOOK

Project editor   Michele Byam
Managing art editor   Jane Owen
Special photography
Colin Keates
(Natural History
Museum, London),
Kim Taylor
and Dave King

Editorial consultants
Paul Whalley and
the staff of the Natural History Museum

Swallowtail butterfly
Papilio machaon
(North America,
Europe & Asia)

This Eyewitness ® Guide has been
conceived by Dorling Kindersley Limited
and Editions Gallimard

First published in Great Britain in 1988
by Dorling Kindersley Limited
9 Henrietta Street, London WC2E 8PS

12 13 14 15 16 17 18 19 20

White Satin
moth caterpillar,
Leucoma salicis,
(Europe & Asia)

Geometrid moth, *Rhodophitus simplex*
(South Africa)

Visit us on the World Wide Web at
http://www.dk.com

Roseate Emperor moth, *Euchroa trimeni*
(South Africa)

Privet
Hawkmoth
caterpillar,
Sphinx ligustri
(Europe & Asia)

Pyralid moth,
Ethopia roseilinea
(Southeast Asia)

British Library Cataloguing in publication Data
Butterfly & moth.
1. Butterflies and moths
I. Series
595.78

ISBN 0-86313-319-0

African
Migrant butterfly,
Catopsilia florella
(Africa)

Cloudless Giant
Sulfur butterfly,
Phoebis sennae
(North & Central
America)

Lappet moth,
Gastropacha quercifolia
(Europe & Asia)

Colour reproduction by Colourscan, Singapore
Typeset by Windsor Graphics, Ringwood, Hampshire
Printed in China by Toppan Printing Co., (Shenzhen) Ltd.

Contents

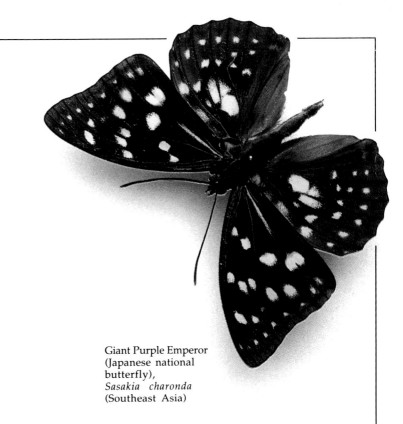

Giant Purple Emperor
(Japanese national
butterfly),
Sasakia charonda
(Southeast Asia)

Butterfly or moth?

BUTTERFLIES AND MOTHS ARE THE MOST POPULAR and easily recognizable of insects. Together, the two groups make up a large group (or Order) of insects known as the Lepidoptera (from the Greek words for "scale" and "wing"). The Order is divided into families of butterflies and moths, containing about 150,000 known species. The division of Lepidoptera into butterflies and moths is an artificial one, based on a number of observable differences. For example, most butterflies fly by day and most moths fly by night; many butterflies are brightly coloured and many moths are dull-coloured; most butterflies hold their wings upright over their backs, while most moths rest with their wings flat; butterfly antennae are knobbed at the tip but moth antennae are either feather-like or plain. But despite these rules, there is not one single feature that separates all butterflies from all moths.

MEDIEVAL BUTTERFLY
A beautifully painted Red Admiral decorates a 16th-century Flemish manuscript, *Hours of Anne of Brittany.*

Wings folded over back

SPOT THE DIFFERENCE
There are several ways to tell which of these two insects is a hawk-moth from Africa, *Euchloron megaera,* and which is a Blue Morpho butterfly, *Morpho peleides,* from Central America. Like many moths, the hawk-moth has a fat abdomen. It also has a moth's typical simple or feathery antennae, rather than the butterfly's club-tipped antennae. And if you had a magnifying glass, you could see that only the moth has a tiny hook and bristle linking its fore wings and hind wings.

Antenna without club

Fat abdomen

A short life, but a long history

It seems strange to think of graceful moths flying about giant dinosaurs, but from fossils we can tell that the first primitive moths lived about 140 million years ago. Butterflies evolved later than moths, the oldest fossils discovered so far being about 40 million years old. By the time the first people appeared, about five million years ago, butterflies and moths were like those we see today.

AMERICAN PIONEER *left*
This 40-million-year old specimen of a Nymphalid butterfly, *Prodryas persephone,* was found in the fossil beds of Lake Florissant, Colorado.

EGYPTIAN TOMB PAINTING
The ancient Egyptians believed that in the afterworld the dead could still hunt birds and see butterflies by the banks of the River Nile.

Lepidoptera versus the rest

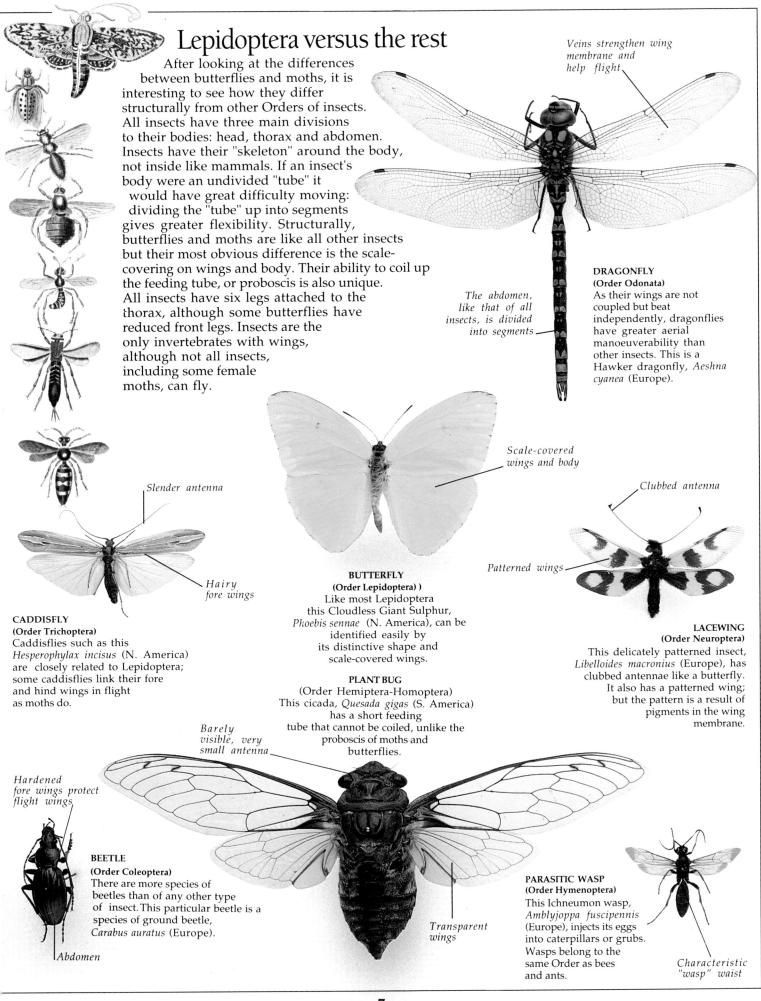

After looking at the differences between butterflies and moths, it is interesting to see how they differ structurally from other Orders of insects. All insects have three main divisions to their bodies: head, thorax and abdomen. Insects have their "skeleton" around the body, not inside like mammals. If an insect's body were an undivided "tube" it would have great difficulty moving: dividing the "tube" up into segments gives greater flexibility. Structurally, butterflies and moths are like all other insects but their most obvious difference is the scale-covering on wings and body. Their ability to coil up the feeding tube, or proboscis is also unique. All insects have six legs attached to the thorax, although some butterflies have reduced front legs. Insects are the only invertebrates with wings, although not all insects, including some female moths, can fly.

Veins strengthen wing membrane and help flight

The abdomen, like that of all insects, is divided into segments

DRAGONFLY
(Order Odonata)
As their wings are not coupled but beat independently, dragonflies have greater aerial manoeuverability than other insects. This is a Hawker dragonfly, *Aeshna cyanea* (Europe).

Scale-covered wings and body

Slender antenna

Hairy fore wings

CADDISFLY
(Order Trichoptera)
Caddisflies such as this *Hesperophylax incisus* (N. America) are closely related to Lepidoptera; some caddisflies link their fore and hind wings in flight as moths do.

BUTTERFLY
(Order Lepidoptera))
Like most Lepidoptera this Cloudless Giant Sulphur, *Phoebis sennae* (N. America), can be identified easily by its distinctive shape and scale-covered wings.

PLANT BUG
(Order Hemiptera-Homoptera)
This cicada, *Quesada gigas* (S. America) has a short feeding tube that cannot be coiled, unlike the proboscis of moths and butterflies.

Clubbed antenna

Patterned wings

LACEWING
(Order Neuroptera)
This delicately patterned insect, *Libelloides macronius* (Europe), has clubbed antennae like a butterfly. It also has a patterned wing; but the pattern is a result of pigments in the wing membrane.

Barely visible, very small antenna

Hardened fore wings protect flight wings

BEETLE
(Order Coleoptera)
There are more species of beetles than of any other type of insect. This particular beetle is a species of ground beetle, *Carabus auratus* (Europe).

Abdomen

Transparent wings

PARASITIC WASP
(Order Hymenoptera)
This Ichneumon wasp, *Amblyjoppa fuscipennis* (Europe), injects its eggs into caterpillars or grubs. Wasps belong to the same Order as bees and ants.

Characteristic "wasp" waist

The life of a butterfly

THE LIFE CYCLE OF A BUTTERFLY OR MOTH consists of four different stages: egg, caterpillar, pupa and adult. The length of the life cycle, from egg to adult, varies enormously between species. It may be as little as a few weeks if the insect lives in the high temperatures of buildings such as grain stores, like some of the Pyralid moths. Other moths may live for several years. Sometimes most of the cycle takes place concealed from human view. For example, most of the life cycle of the leaf-mining moths takes place between the upper and lower surfaces of a single leaf, with only the adult emerging into the outside world. In the same way, some of the wood-boring larvae of the Cossid moths may spend months, or even years in the caterpillar stage, hidden inside a tree. Other species pass their entire life cycle much more exposed. These are usually either well camouflaged, or distasteful to predators. There are many variations on the life-cycle - some species, for example, having fewer moults in the caterpillar stage than others. These two pages illustrate the life cycle of a South American Owl Butterfly, *Caligo beltrao* (also pp. 16, 23, 35).

Young caterpillar with new, green skin

Older caterpillar with brown skin is about to pupate

1 EGGS
The eggs of the Owl Butterfly have delicate ribs that meet at the top. The ribbing and the structure of the shell (a tough coating like an insect's body, not a brittle one like a hen's egg) are designed to protect the egg from water loss while allowing it to "breathe" (pp. 12-13).

2 CATERPILLARS
Once the caterpillar hatches, it feeds and grows rapidly. It moults its restrictive skin, developing a new one underneath, which stretches and allows new growth after the moult. Some species of *Caligo* are pests on bananas in Central and South America. The long, slender shape of the caterpillar helps to conceal it against the midrib of the leaves on which it feeds (p. 16).

MEAT-EATING MOTH *left*
The pyralid *Laetilia coccicidivora* (N. & S. America) has a similar life-cycle to other moths (pp. 36-37). It differs in the feeding habits of the caterpillar, which is predatory and eats scale insects and greenfly that it catches as it moves across the plant.

SILK SPINNER *right*
The life-cycle of the Wild Silkmoth, *Samia cynthia* (India), shows all the typical stages, but since it is a moth, it spins a cocoon in which to pupate (pp. 38-39). The caterpillar of this moth feeds on a variety of plants, including the Castor-oil plant, *Ricinus* (right). It also spins a dense cocoon.

WINTER SLEEPERS

The Hop Merchant or Comma, *Polygonia comma* (N. America), and the Comma, *Polygonia c-album* (Europe & Asia) are closely related Nymphalid butterflies (p. 29). Their caterpillars feed on nettles, *Urtica*, and hops, *Humulus*, and the adult butterflies, which emerge in late summer and autumn, hibernate during winter in their adult stage (p. 51).

Comma caterpillar

Comma chrysalis

Comma butterfly gets its name from the small white C-shape on its wing

Comma with wings open, showing its rich brown and orange patterning

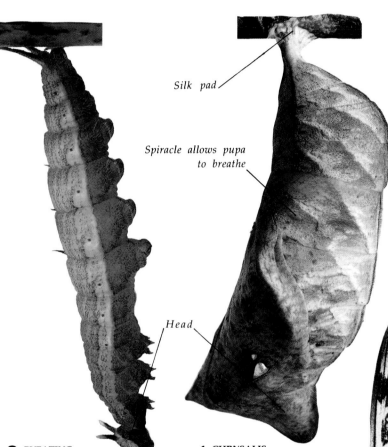

Silk pad

Spiracle allows pupa to breathe

Head

3 PUPATING

By this stage (pp. 20-21) the caterpillar has darkened slightly and, using the silk from the spinneret under its head, has applied a small silken pad to the plant. It attaches its hind claspers firmly to this and hangs, head down, from the stem. Underneath its skin, the skin of the next stage, the chrysalis, is forming. Gradually, with much wriggling and twisting, it will slough off its caterpillar skin and shake it away - legs, head, and all - so that the completed chrysalis is revealed.

4 CHRYSALIS

The chrysalis (pp. 22-23), now completely formed, does not have any external legs or antennae. Inside the chrysalis, the body of the caterpillar is broken down, special cells take over the insect's development and gradually the adult is formed. The change from the caterpillar to the butterfly that finally emerges is one of the most remarkable events in the natural world. The oval structure on each body segment is called a spiracle and allows the chrysalis to breathe - although externally inactive, it needs energy for all the changes taking place inside.

5 ADULT *below*

The adult butterfly, so totally unlike the early feeding stages, has emerged, spread its wings and is ready to fly (p. 35). Adult butterflies often live for only a few weeks, although a few species may survive for a year. After a time their wings often become noticeably tattered from general wear and tear; they can still fly with ragged wings, although less efficiently than before. The adult's role in the life cycle is to reproduce and disperse its eggs where they will be most likely to survive. Adult butterflies seek out new areas to colonize and many can fly long distances. Generally they mate as soon as possible after they emerge (pp. 10-11).

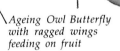

Ageing Owl Butterfly with ragged wings feeding on fruit

Courtship and egg laying

THE MOST IMPORTANT EVENTS in the lives of butterflies and moths are mating and the laying of eggs. The striking colours and shapes of many species are thought to attract the opposite sex; in addition, most butterflies and moths have complicated courtship behaviour. As well as performing elaborate courtship flights and "dances", they often use chemicals called pheromones to attract members of the opposite sex. "Assembling" - the attraction of males to females by scent - is now known to be due to these chemicals. In butterflies it is usually the male who produces these powerful scents, while in moths it is often the female. When a male finds a female who shows an interest in him, they both land. The female holds her wings in a partly open position so that the male can land easily alongside her and continue spreading his scent. The mating pair will often tap one another with their antennae, detecting other scents which stimulate activity at close range. Mating may last for about twenty minutes, or for several hours, during which time the two insects remain immobile.

A 19th-century version of the butterflies' courtship dance

Female Lackey Moth

FROM EGG TO CATERPILLAR
This moth, *Malacosoma neustria* (Europe), has a hairy caterpillar that eats the leaves of many trees. The moth's eggs are shown on the opposite page.

Male Sweet Oil butterfly

Female Sweet Oil butterfly

BUTTERFLIES MATING
Like this pair of Sweet Oil butterflies, *Mechanitis polymnia* (S. America), most butterflies mate on a plant. They can fly while linked together, but they avoid this unless disturbed so as not to become more conspicuous. After mating, males look for another female, but the mated females seek out the food plant of the caterpillars. Although a few butterflies, notably those with grass-feeding larvae, scatter their eggs, most females actively look for a particular plant.

A TWO-HEADED BUTTERFLY?
A mating pair, like these two Asian swallowtails, can look like a two-headed butterfly. The tail-to-tail position links the genitalia of male and female together. The male has a complicated series of structures including claspers, which he uses to grasp the female's abdomen. The genital organs of butterflies and moths are a useful way of identifying species.

Female swallowtail

Male swallowtail

SEXUAL DIFFERENCES *right and below right*
The males and females of some butterfly species are widely different in external appearance, a condition known as sexual dimorphism. An example is the Orange-tip, *Anthocharis cardamines* (Europe & Asia), in which the males have a distinctive orange colour on the wing-tips, while the females have black wing-tips. In some species the females are larger than the males, while a few female moths are flightless (p. 30).

Male Orange-tip has brightly coloured orange wing-tips

Female Orange-tip has black wing-tips

Egg laying

After selecting the correct plant for the caterpillars, the female walks over a leaf, testing it carefully, presumably to make sure it belongs to the right plant species. We know that many species can detect chemicals from different plants: cabbage-eating Large and Small White butterflies, *Pieris brassicae* (Europe) and *Pieris rapae* (Europe, N. America & Australia), have been persuaded to lay eggs on plants that their caterpillars will not eat, by putting traces of extract from cabbages on the surface of the leaves.

SILKMOTH LAYING EGGS *left*
This female silkmoth has laid her batch of eggs on a mulberrry leaf. Although this moth may lay many eggs in the wild, few of them will become adults. But in artificial conditions, large numbers of moths can be raised from one egg batch (see pp. 40-41).

DELICATE OPERATION
This Pierid butterfly from Central America, *Perrhybris pyrra*, is laying its eggs on the upper surface of the leaf. She is very vulnerable to disturbance here, and a heavy rainstorm will interrupt egg laying.

Egg

SITES FOR EGG LAYING
Some species of *Heliconius* butterflies lay their eggs on tendrils of the passion flower (above). The Lackey Moth (see opposite page) lays its eggs in a ring around a twig, so that they look like part of the plant (below).

Eggs

ABOUT TO HATCH *right*
These eggs of the Blue Mormon butterfly, *Papilio polymnestor* (Asia), have darkened and are about to hatch. Soon tiny caterpillars will emerge (p. 18). A Blue Mormon lays its eggs in a random pattern rather than a cluster, so there is more chance that predatory bugs will overlook some of them.

Egg under leaf

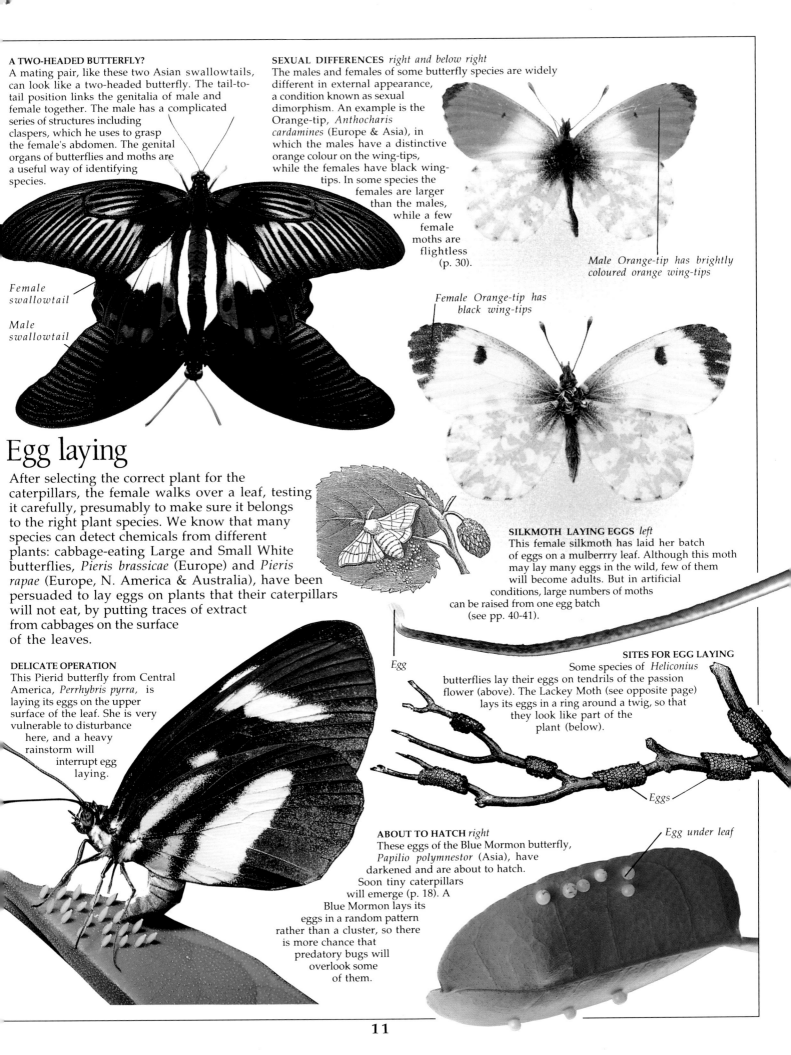

An emerging caterpillar

Bᴜᴛᴛᴇʀꜰʟɪᴇꜱ ᴀɴᴅ ᴍᴏᴛʜꜱ usually lay large numbers of eggs. The number varies greatly; some females lay over 1,000, although only a few eggs may survive to become adults. Eggs vary greatly from one species to another in their colour and in their surface texture, which can be smooth or beautifully sculptured. The two main types are a flattened oval shape, usually with a smooth surface, and a more upright shape, which often has a heavily ribbed surface. In most cases the female lays the eggs on a leaf or stem (see pp. 10-11), but some species - particularly the grass-feeding butterflies - simply release their eggs in flight. Both methods are designed to place the caterpillar as near as possible to the plant on which it feeds. These two pages show a caterpillar of a South American Owl Butterfly (see pp. 8-9, 16, 23, and 25) hatching from its egg.

THE EGGS IN POSITION
The Owl Butterfly lays its eggs in groups. The colour of the individual eggs can vary in this species. They turn darker as the time of hatching gets near.

Actual size of egg

Pattern of ridges can be a useful aid to identification of eggs

RESTING
In many temperate butterflies and moths, autumn-laid eggs usually go into a resting stage called "diapause", to pass the winter. This state is broken by low or fluctuating temperatures.

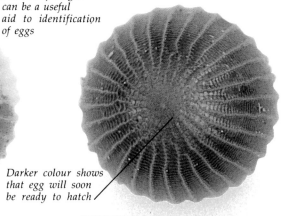

Darker colour shows that egg will soon be ready to hatch

WARMING UP
Once winter diapause has broken, and the temperature has risen enough for the caterpillar to stand a chance of survival, the egg darkens in colour as the tiny caterpillar gets ready to emerge.

CUTTING A CIRCLE
In order to hatch, the caterpillar must bite its way through the shell of the egg. This is not a hard, brittle shell like that of a hen's egg, but it still poses a tough task for the minute caterpillar: its jaws have to cut a circle big enough for the head to come out.

Head of caterpillar starting to appear

Opening where caterpillar's jaws have cut through egg shell

Ocelli

Antenna

EMERGING HEAD-FIRST
The caterpillar seems to have a disproportionately large head and jaws, but the enormous mouthparts are useful for biting an opening in the egg shell. Nevertheless, it can be quite difficult for the small caterpillar to extract itself from the egg head-first. The dark spots on each side of the head are simple eyes called ocelli. The caterpillar also gets information about its surroundings from its tiny antennae.

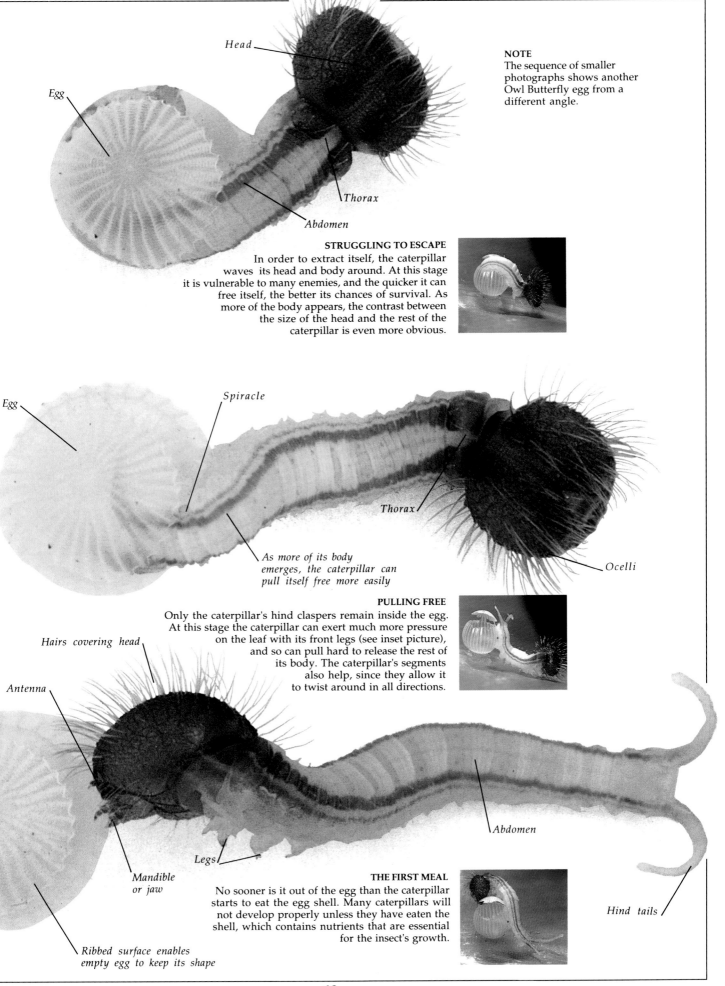

Head

Egg

Thorax

Abdomen

NOTE
The sequence of smaller photographs shows another Owl Butterfly egg from a different angle.

STRUGGLING TO ESCAPE
In order to extract itself, the caterpillar waves its head and body around. At this stage it is vulnerable to many enemies, and the quicker it can free itself, the better its chances of survival. As more of the body appears, the contrast between the size of the head and the rest of the caterpillar is even more obvious.

Egg

Spiracle

Thorax

Ocelli

As more of its body emerges, the caterpillar can pull itself free more easily

PULLING FREE
Only the caterpillar's hind claspers remain inside the egg. At this stage the caterpillar can exert much more pressure on the leaf with its front legs (see inset picture), and so can pull hard to release the rest of its body. The caterpillar's segments also help, since they allow it to twist around in all directions.

Hairs covering head

Antenna

Abdomen

Legs

Mandible or jaw

Hind tails

Ribbed surface enables empty egg to keep its shape

THE FIRST MEAL
No sooner is it out of the egg than the caterpillar starts to eat the egg shell. Many caterpillars will not develop properly unless they have eaten the shell, which contains nutrients that are essential for the insect's growth.

Caterpillars

IT IS A PITY THAT THE CATERPILLAR is usually dismissed simply as a "feeding tube" because it is a complex and interesting stage in the life-cycle of a butterfly or moth. Caterpillars carry in their bodies the cells that eventually produce an adult insect. They moult several times during their life, discarding their outer skin to reveal a new, more elastic, skin in which they can grow. Caterpillars are usually very active during this stage and need food and oxygen to grow and sustain themselves. But they do not have lungs like mammals. They take in air through small holes called spiracles in the side of their bodies. The air passes along fine tubes, or tracheoles, from which the oxygen is extracted by the body fluid. Caterpillars have a nervous system with a primitive "brain", or cerebral ganglion, in the head. The head itself is equipped with sense organs to tell the caterpillar what is going on in the world around it. These include short antennae and often a half-circle of simple, light-sensitive "eyes", or ocelli. Also on the head are the massive jaws needed for chewing plant food. An essential feature of caterpillars, not present in the adult, is their ability to produce silk from special glands, and to force it out through a spinneret under the head (pp. 40-41).

The Caterpillar talking to Alice from *Alice in Wonderland* by Lewis Carroll

Spine or horn at tip of abdomen

Abdomen

Anal clasper

Four pairs of prolegs

CATERPILLAR OF DEATH'S-HEAD HAWK-MOTH (adult moth below)

BEDSTRAW HAWK-MOTH *right*
The caterpillar of the Bedstraw Hawk-moth, *Celerio galii*, feeds, as its name implies, on the Bedstraw plant, *Galium*. The moth is found all over Europe and Asia, although it does not overwinter in the more northerly parts. Similar North American species include the tomato pest known as the Tobacco Hornworm or Carolina Sphinx, *Manduca sexta*.

ADULT
The Death's-head Hawk-moth, *Acherontia atropos* (Europe, Asia & Africa), gets its name from the skull-like marking on its thorax. The adult moth (also p. 43) has the ability to squeak if handled, whereas the caterpillar only makes a clicking sound.

FAST EATERS
The caterpillars of the Oak Silkmoth (see below) are very greedy eaters. If they become too numerous they can soon strip a tree.

The caterpillar's body is made of such flexible tissue that it can easily twist itself around

Head

Half-eaten oak leaf

Claspers

Fading colour indicates that this caterpillar is about to pupate

SOFT BUT SECURE *left*
Most birds and other predators avoid hairy caterpillars like this one, but some birds, such as the European Cuckoo, specialize in eating them and do not worry about their hairs!

INCHWORM *right*
Inchworms are caterpillars of the group of Geometrid moths called loopers (Europe, Asia, N. & S. America). They have lost most of their prolegs, and move by looping along (also p. 43).

STEM-DWELLER *above*
The caterpillar of the Squash-bug, *Melittia cucurbitae* (N. America), bores into the stems of squashes, where it can be a pest. This conceals the caterpillar and protects it from the weather.

ON THE MARCH *right*
The caterpillars of the Pine Processionary Moth, *Thaumetopoea pityocampa* (Europe & Africa), follow one another in a head-to-tail line to find a new food plant.

The caterpillar of the Death's-head Hawk-moth feeds on potato leaves and can at times be a pest

Thorax

Head

Antenna

Spinneret

Spiracle

Three pairs of legs on thorax

SUSPENDED IN MID-AIR
This caterpillar is attaching itself to a twig before pupating. From the spinneret under its head it has spun a pad of silk on the stem and is now hanging head downwards. The way the caterpillar curls suggests its active movement as the pupa is formed under its skin.

Small antenna

Labial palp

Jaws

MIGHTY JAWS *left and right*
Close-up views of the head of the Oak Silkmoth caterpillar, *Antheraea harti*, (also pp. 62-63) show how large the jaws are in relation to the head as a whole. This emphasizes their importance to the caterpillar from the moment it leaves the egg (pp. 12-13). The palps are sensitive organs that are probably used to identify food.

Exotic caterpillars

WOOLLY BEARS *left and below*
The long hairs of many Arctiid moths - "woolly bears" - can cause allergic reactions in some people.

Aᴘᴀʀᴛ ꜰʀᴏᴍ ʙᴇɪɴɢ ᴇꜰꜰɪᴄɪᴇɴᴛ ᴀᴛ ꜰᴇᴇᴅɪɴɢ and growing, caterpillars must be able to survive in a hostile world. While caterpillars are an essential food source for birds to feed their young, it is clearly a disadvantage to be on the daily menu. This is why caterpillars have adopted a large variety of shapes and protective devices in order to survive. The caterpillars shown on the next four pages all come from tropical countries (see pp. 32-35 and 44-47) where, as in all wild places, "eat or be eaten" is very much the rule. Not only birds and mammals, but certain predatory insects relish a juicy caterpillar. Fortunately for the caterpillars, many tropical species feed on plants whose contents may be poisonous. By absorbing the poisons and advertising their distastefulness by their bright colours, great numbers of caterpillars avoid an early death.

Owl Butterfly,
Caligo beltrao,
(S. & C. America)

These caterpillars are not fully grown (Owl caterpillars also on p. 8)

Flambeau,
Dryas iulia,
(N., C. &
S. America)

TINY TIGER
Like its relative the Monarch, the brightly coloured caterpillar of the Plain Tiger likes to advertise its presence. It is possible that the filaments sticking out of the caterpillar's body give it further protection by dispersing an unpleasant smell.

Plain Tiger,
Danaus chrysippus,
(Africa,
S. E. Asia &
Australia)

GROUP OF OWLS
The colouring of these Owl Butterfly caterpillars (also pp. 8-9) makes them less conspicuous along the rib of the plant. The caterpillars have a series of filaments at their heads and tails that probably help to break up their outline.

Bright stripes act as a warning to its enemies

Monarch,
Danaus plexippus,
(Australia, N. & S. America)

Species of passionflower (Passiflora)

Filaments

Zebra, *Heliconius charitonius* (N., C. & S. America)

WARNINGLY COLOURED
Monarch caterpillars can retain poisonous substances from their milkweed and dogbane food plants. Once a bird has pecked one of these caterpillars, it will usually avoid other Monarchs.

SOLITARY FEEDER
The caterpillar of the Great Eggfly, a species of butterfly found in Asia and in the Pacific region, feeds on a range of plants as diverse as mallow and types of daisy. Adult Great Eggflies often mimic distasteful species of butterfly in order to protect themselves (see pp. 56-57 on mimicry).

An adult female
Great Eggfly butterfly

"Warning" red stripes usually indicate a poisonous caterpillar

Great Eggfly,
Hypolimnas bolina,
(S. E. Asia &
Australia)

Caterpillar armed with long spines characteristic of Heliconiidae caterpillars

Flambeau caterpillar

DISTASTEFUL GANG
Among the most beautifully coloured butterflies, Heliconiines (sometimes called longwings) occur in the southern United States, and Central and South America. Like all Heliconiines, the caterpillars of these three species feed on poisonous passionflower vines.

An adult Postman
butterfly

An adult Flambeau
butterfly

DANGEROUS GROUP
It is thought that the caterpillars of the Sweet Oil butterfly, *Mechanitis polymnia* (S. America), absorb poisonous substances from the leaves of the deadly nightshade plants they feed on. Although the poisons are harmless to the caterpillar or adult butterfly, they are extremely distasteful to a bird or any other enemy.

Postman caterpillar

Adult Sweet Oil
butterfly

Postman,
Heliconius melpomene
(S. America)

Unlike many species of caterpillar, Sweet Oils like to feed in a group

SWALLOWTAIL DEFENCE
The caterpillars of many swallowtail butterflies have a Y-shaped organ behind their heads. When the caterpillar is disturbed, it thrusts out two finger-like glands, rather like pushing out the fingers of a glove, that emit an unpleasant smell.

Common Mormon,
Papilio polytes,
(S. E. Asia)

Y-shaped organ known as osmeterium is behind the caterpillar's head but not visible in the photograph

Some swallowtail caterpillars rear up in a threatening manner if disturbed

Sweet Oil,
Mechanitis polymnia,
(S. America)

Continued on next page

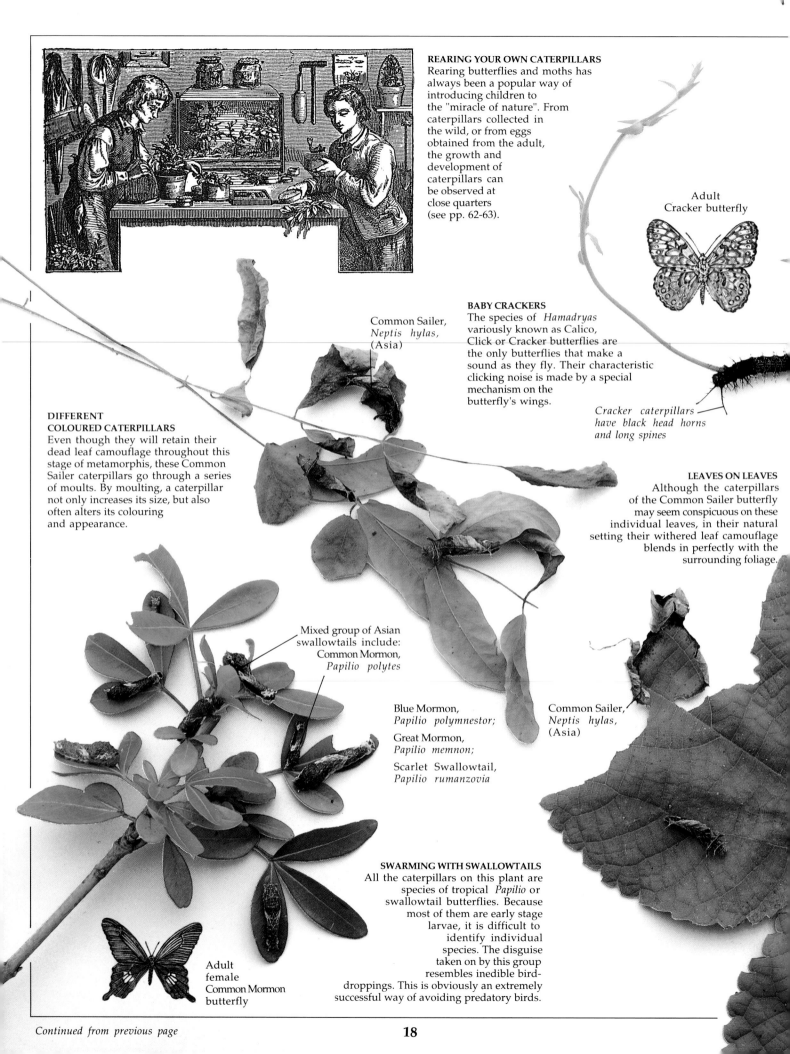

REARING YOUR OWN CATERPILLARS
Rearing butterflies and moths has always been a popular way of introducing children to the "miracle of nature". From caterpillars collected in the wild, or from eggs obtained from the adult, the growth and development of caterpillars can be observed at close quarters (see pp. 62-63).

Adult
Cracker butterfly

Common Sailer,
Neptis hylas,
(Asia)

BABY CRACKERS
The species of *Hamadryas* variously known as Calico, Click or Cracker butterflies are the only butterflies that make a sound as they fly. Their characteristic clicking noise is made by a special mechanism on the butterfly's wings.

Cracker caterpillars have black head horns and long spines

DIFFERENT COLOURED CATERPILLARS
Even though they will retain their dead leaf camouflage throughout this stage of metamorphis, these Common Sailer caterpillars go through a series of moults. By moulting, a caterpillar not only increases its size, but also often alters its colouring and appearance.

LEAVES ON LEAVES
Although the caterpillars of the Common Sailer butterfly may seem conspicuous on these individual leaves, in their natural setting their withered leaf camouflage blends in perfectly with the surrounding foliage.

Mixed group of Asian swallowtails include:
Common Mormon,
Papilio polytes

Blue Mormon,
Papilio polymnestor;

Great Mormon,
Papilio memnon;

Scarlet Swallowtail,
Papilio rumanzovia

Common Sailer,
Neptis hylas,
(Asia)

SWARMING WITH SWALLOWTAILS
All the caterpillars on this plant are species of tropical *Papilio* or swallowtail butterflies. Because most of them are early stage larvae, it is difficult to identify individual species. The disguise taken on by this group resembles inedible bird-droppings. This is obviously an extremely successful way of avoiding predatory birds.

Adult
female
Common Mormon
butterfly

A MOTH AMONG MANY
Among the tropical caterpillars on these pages, the Silver-striped Hawk-moth is the only moth. For protection it has a black horn at its end and a fearsome look, with large yellow-ringed "eyes" on its back.

Has the characteristic horn of hawk-moth caterpillars - really a harmless long spine

Silver-striped Hawk-moth, *Hippotion celerio*, (Europe, Africa, Asia & Australia)

Adult Silver-striped Hawk-moth

Leopard, *Phalanta phalantha*, (Africa & Asia)

Cracker, *Hamadryas amphinome*, (C. & S. America)

Cracker, *Hamadryas feronia*, (C. & S. America, sometimes Texas)

LEOPARDS WITHOUT SPOTS
Although they don't look very aggressive, the popular name for this African species of butterfly is the Leopard. Like the *Heliconius* caterpillars on pages 16 and 17, Leopards are members of the Nymphalid family, recognizable at the caterpillar stage for their spiny appearance.

MEAL FOR A LIZARD
Although it looks as though it is about to fall victim to a hungry lizard, the caterpillar may still be able to escape if it is distasteful or spiny. It might even drop to the ground to escape the lizard.

Cracker, (U.S. Guatemalan Calico), *Hamadryas guatemalena*, (C. America & sometimes Texas)

Caterpillar to pupa

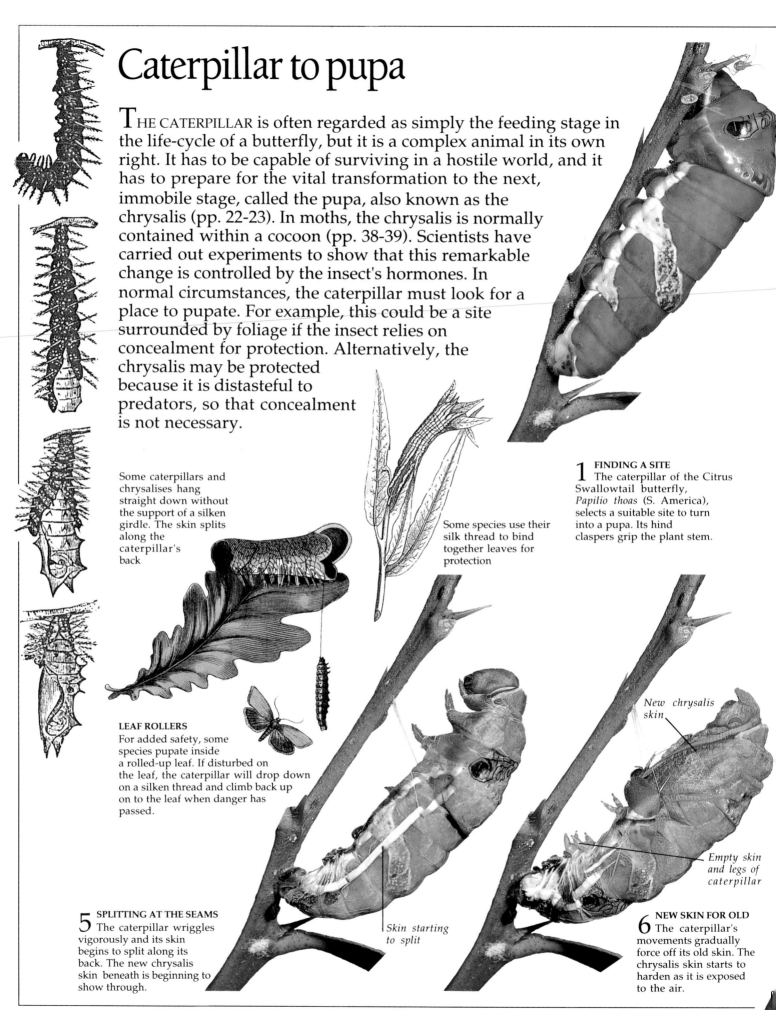

THE CATERPILLAR is often regarded as simply the feeding stage in the life-cycle of a butterfly, but it is a complex animal in its own right. It has to be capable of surviving in a hostile world, and it has to prepare for the vital transformation to the next, immobile stage, called the pupa, also known as the chrysalis (pp. 22-23). In moths, the chrysalis is normally contained within a cocoon (pp. 38-39). Scientists have carried out experiments to show that this remarkable change is controlled by the insect's hormones. In normal circumstances, the caterpillar must look for a place to pupate. For example, this could be a site surrounded by foliage if the insect relies on concealment for protection. Alternatively, the chrysalis may be protected because it is distasteful to predators, so that concealment is not necessary.

Some caterpillars and chrysalises hang straight down without the support of a silken girdle. The skin splits along the caterpillar's back

Some species use their silk thread to bind together leaves for protection

1 FINDING A SITE
The caterpillar of the Citrus Swallowtail butterfly, *Papilio thoas* (S. America), selects a suitable site to turn into a pupa. Its hind claspers grip the plant stem.

LEAF ROLLERS
For added safety, some species pupate inside a rolled-up leaf. If disturbed on the leaf, the caterpillar will drop down on a silken thread and climb back up on to the leaf when danger has passed.

New chrysalis skin

Empty skin and legs of caterpillar

5 SPLITTING AT THE SEAMS
The caterpillar wriggles vigorously and its skin begins to split along its back. The new chrysalis skin beneath is beginning to show through.

Skin starting to split

6 NEW SKIN FOR OLD
The caterpillar's movements gradually force off its old skin. The chrysalis skin starts to harden as it is exposed to the air.

Hind claspers

Thread of silk to make girdle

Spinneret produces silk

Tail of pupa secure on silken pad

2 STARTING TO SPIN
The caterpillar has turned head down and is producing silk from the spinneret below its head. The caterpillar weaves this silk into a small pad which it attaches to the plant.

3 MAKING THE GIRDLE
Having turned around again, the caterpillar spins while moving its head from side to side, producing a girdle around its body with the silk from its spinneret.

4 HANGING ON
The caterpillar is now attached to the stem by its hind claspers and the silk girdle. Under its skin, the chrysalis is already starting to form.

7 A FIRM GRIP
The pupa works its tail hooks into the silken pad that it had earlier spun as a caterpillar.

8 THE COMPLETED CHRYSALIS
In its final form, the chrysalis looks like a leaf. It is still attached to the twig by the silken girdle and pad.

The pupa stage

THE PUPA IS THE THIRD MAJOR STAGE in a butterfly or moth's life. This is when it is transformed from a caterpillar into an adult. A butterfly pupa is usually called a chrysalis and, depending on the species and climate, it remains in this form for weeks or even months. Except for an occasional twitch, the pupa seems lifeless, but in fact amazing changes are taking place, some of which can eventually be seen through the pupal skin. Because a pupa cannot move about, the insect is far more vulnerable to predators at this time than when it is a caterpillar or adult. For the majority of pupae their best hope of survival is to adapt their shape and colour to their surroundings. The exceptions are the more brightly coloured pupae which, being poisonous, are only too happy to advertise their presence. Many moths pupate underground, but few butterfly chrysalids have this added protection. Looking at the butterfly chrysalids on these pages, we can get some idea of how much they vary in shape and colour.

THE FREAK *below*
As can be seen from these two *Calinaga buddha* (Asia) chrysalids, variation in colour helps them to camouflage themselves on a wide range of backgrounds. The brown form will clearly have a protective advantage on a twig.

Wing veins

THE ARCHDUKE *left*
A close look reveals that the wing veins are visible, showing that the adult *Euthalia dirtea* (S.E. Asia) is almost ready to hatch.

MALAY LACEWING *below*
One of the important rules of camouflage is for the insect to break up its outline. The *Cethosia hypsea* (Asia) chrysalis does this by creating an irregular shape.

Shaped like dead leaf for camouflage

Spiny shape for disguise

CRUISER *left*
The resemblance to a dead and decaying leaf, and the spiny shape, helps protect *Vindula erota* (Asia) from detection by hungry predators.

Bright reflective gold spot distracts predators

Visible wing veins

THE QUEEN *above*
The chrysalis of *Danaus gilippus* (N., C. & S. America) is poisonous to predators. The poison comes from the plant on which the caterpillar feeds.

The swallowtail *Papilio machaon*, (Europe, N. America & Asia), is either green or brown

CRIMSON PATCH LONGWING *left*
As well as an irregular shape, *Heliconius erato* (S. America), has sharp spines along the wing case.

Developing wing

Sharp spines

CLOUDLESS GIANT SULPHUR *right*
The green, leaf-like shape of *Phoebis sennae* (N. & C. America) passes unnoticed in the vegetation of its natural habitat.

Developing wing veins

Pronounced hump in middle

An adult Cloudless Giant Sulphur (see above) beginning to break out of its chrysalis

Developing head

POSTMAN
Closely related to the Crimson Patch Longwing (left), the chrysalis of *Heliconius melpomene* (S. America) is equally well camouflaged and protective in shape.

FLAMBEAU
Dryas julia (C. & S. America) is another dark-brown rugged-looking chrysalis that gains protection from its ability to resemble woody backgrounds.

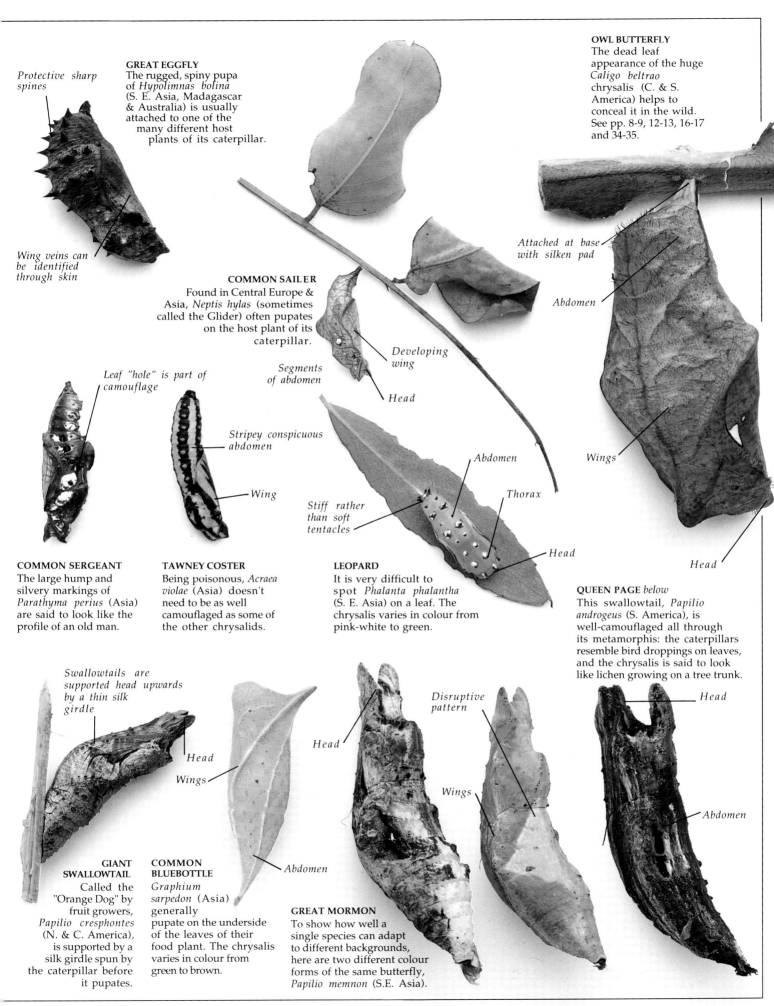

GREAT EGGFLY
The rugged, spiny pupa of *Hypolimnas bolina* (S. E. Asia, Madagascar & Australia) is usually attached to one of the many different host plants of its caterpillar.

Protective sharp spines

Wing veins can be identified through skin

OWL BUTTERFLY
The dead leaf appearance of the huge *Caligo beltrao* chrysalis (C. & S. America) helps to conceal it in the wild. See pp. 8-9, 12-13, 16-17 and 34-35.

Attached at base with silken pad

Abdomen

Wings

Head

COMMON SAILER
Found in Central Europe & Asia, *Neptis hylas* (sometimes called the Glider) often pupates on the host plant of its caterpillar.

Developing wing

Segments of abdomen

Head

Leaf "hole" is part of camouflage

Stripey conspicuous abdomen

Wing

Abdomen

Thorax

Stiff rather than soft tentacles

Head

COMMON SERGEANT
The large hump and silvery markings of *Parathyma perius* (Asia) are said to look like the profile of an old man.

TAWNEY COSTER
Being poisonous, *Acraea violae* (Asia) doesn't need to be as well camouflaged as some of the other chrysalids.

LEOPARD
It is very difficult to spot *Phalanta phalantha* (S. E. Asia) on a leaf. The chrysalis varies in colour from pink-white to green.

QUEEN PAGE *below*
This swallowtail, *Papilio androgeus* (S. America), is well-camouflaged all through its metamorphis: the caterpillars resemble bird droppings on leaves, and the chrysalis is said to look like lichen growing on a tree trunk.

Swallowtails are supported head upwards by a thin silk girdle

Head

Wings

Disruptive pattern

Head

Wings

Head

Abdomen

GIANT SWALLOWTAIL
Called the "Orange Dog" by fruit growers, *Papilio cresphontes* (N. & C. America), is supported by a silk girdle spun by the caterpillar before it pupates.

COMMON BLUEBOTTLE
Graphium sarpedon (Asia) generally pupate on the underside of the leaves of their food plant. The chrysalis varies in colour from green to brown.

Abdomen

GREAT MORMON
To show how well a single species can adapt to different backgrounds, here are two different colour forms of the same butterfly, *Papilio memnon* (S.E. Asia).

23

An emerging butterfly

AS IT CHANGES FROM AN EGG TO AN ADULT a butterfly renews itself on several different occasions. When the growing stages (metamorphis) are over, all that remains is for the chrysalis to crack open and the adult to emerge. Within the virtually immobile chrysalis such tremendous changes have taken place that when this happens a new creature appears to be born. The emerging butterfly shown here is a Blue Morpho, *Morpho peleides*, from Central and South America.

"The Flight into Egypt", from an illuminated manuscript, the *Hastings Hours*, c. 1480

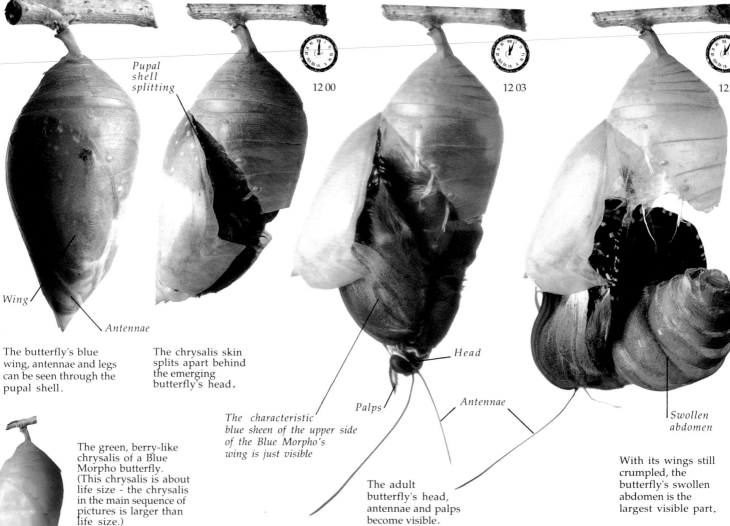

Pupal shell splitting

12 00

12 03

12 05

Wing

Antennae

The butterfly's blue wing, antennae and legs can be seen through the pupal shell.

The chrysalis skin splits apart behind the emerging butterfly's head.

The green, berry-like chrysalis of a Blue Morpho butterfly. (This chrysalis is about life size - the chrysalis in the main sequence of pictures is larger than life size.)

The characteristic blue sheen of the upper side of the Blue Morpho's wing is just visible

Head

Palps

Antennae

The adult butterfly's head, antennae and palps (sensory organs for tasting food) become visible.

Swollen abdomen

With its wings still crumpled, the butterfly's swollen abdomen is the largest visible part.

1 READY TO HATCH
Hours before emerging, the butterfly is still developing. By now, some of the Blue Morpho's structures can be seen through the skin of the chrysalis. The dark area is the butterfly's wing, and traces of the antennae and legs are visible towards the bottom of the chrysalis. It takes about eighty-five days after the egg is laid for a Blue Morpho adult to emerge.

2 FIRST STAGE
Once the insect has completed its metamorphis and is ready to emerge, it begins to pump body fluids into its head and thorax. This helps to split the chrysalis along certain weak points, so that the adult insect can begin to force its way out with its legs.

3 HEAD AND THORAX EMERGE
Once the the skin of the chrysalis is broken, expansion can proceed more rapidly. Inflation is due not only to the body fluids in the head and thorax, but also to the air the insect takes in. Although by now the antennae, head and palps (sensory organs for tasting food) are visible, the wings are still too soft and crumpled for proper identification.

4 COMPLETELY FREE
Having pushed its way out of the chrysalis, the butterfly's body now hangs free. At this stage, the butterfly's exoskeleton (the outside skeleton of all insects) is soft and still capable of more expansion. If, for any reason, the butterfly is damaged at this stage, or confined (perhaps by a thoughtless collector), complete expansion is not possible: all the parts harden and a crippled butterfly results.

5 STEADILY GROWING WINGS

With the butterfly now out of its pupal skin, the most important actions are the ejection of stored wastes from the abdomen and the expansion of the wings. As it forces blood from its body into its wings, a butterfly or moth will usually hang head-up so that the pull of gravity helps to stretch the crumpled wings.

6 BECOMING ITS FULL SIZE

By now the veins in the wings have almost filled with blood, and it is possible to see the wings visibly expanding. The expansion must take place fairly rapidly, or the wings will dry before they have got to their full size. If this happens the butterfly may be too crippled to fly.

FLY AWAY BUTTERFLY
An adult Blue Morpho butterfly, showing how the upper surface's dazzling blue sheen contrasts so vividly with the brown, spotted underside seen in the picture below (also p. 37).

2 20

7 WAITING TO FLY

After a period of about ten to twenty minutes, the wings reach their full size. The butterfly now waits for its wings to harden properly before it attempts to fly. Then, after an hour or so, and some preliminary opening and closing of its wings, the butterfly takes to the air. It usually flies straight to a plant or other food source for its first meal.

12 07

Legs

Head

Butterflies and moths can cling to surfaces by the claws on the tip of their legs

12 12

Curled proboscis

Palps

Head

12 20

In many cases these droplets are red not yellow, which was probably why people in medieval times claimed that butterflies produced a "rain of blood"

The wing is like a bag that would expand into a balloon if it were not for tiny ligaments that hold the upper and lower membranes together

Wing veins with blood pumped into them

Once the butterfly has pushed its way clear of the chrysalis with its legs, it gets rid of excretory liquid collected during the pupal stage.

The butterfly's wing patterns are now clearly visible, as are its head, palps and proboscis.

The butterfly waits with its wings held apart while they dry and harden. If it is evening, it will rest until the following day before it flies.

Butterflies

BUTTERFLIES AND MOTHS are unique among insects in that every part of their body, from their wings to their feet, is covered by thousands of delicate scales. The most noticeable scales are those covering the upper and under surfaces of the wings, as these give the butterfly its colour and pattern. The head has two jointed sensory organs called antennae, used for smelling, and a specialized coiled feeding tube, or proboscis, that uncoils when the insect wishes to feed. The two large compound eyes are made up of a large number of individual lenses, or facets. The facets are sensitive not only to movement, but also to the colour patterns of flowers and other butterflies. Divided into three segments, the thorax is the powerhouse of the body, with connecting muscles for the two pairs of wings and the three pairs of segmented legs. The insect's reproductive organs are in the tip of the abdomen, the rest of which contains most of its digestive system.

A Clouded Yellow, *Colias croceus* (Europe), in flight

Feeding habits

All butterflies and most moths have a proboscis (hollow feeding tube), used for drawing up energy-rich nectar, water, and other liquids. A few large moths do not feed as adults but live on food stored up by the larva (pp. 36-37). There are species of butterflies who enjoy sipping the juice of rotting fruit or the sap oozing from trees; others eat honey dew, or the liquids from dead animal carcasses.

Front of head

Labial palps (sensory feelers for testing food suitability)

Proboscis

Close-up of the head of a Pearl-bordered Fritillary, *Clossiana euphrosyne* (Europe)

These fritillary butterflies belong to one of the largest and most colourful butterfly families, the Nymphalidae

Compound eye

Labial palps

Antenna

Coiled proboscis

"TONGUE" SECTION *above*
A magnified cross-section of the proboscis. Situated underneath the head, this hollow feeding tube acts like a tightly coiled drinking straw.

A DRINK AT THE CLUB
It is quite a common sight, especially in hot climates, to see a group of male butterflies drinking from damp soil - possibly to obtain minerals. The majority of the butterflies in this "mud-puddle" club are Bluebottles, *Graphium sarpedon*, from Malaysia.

**HOMERUS
SWALLOWTAIL,
PAPILIO HOMERUS
(JAMAICA)**

Fore wing

Hind wing

RESTING POSITION *left*
In this old engraving, a Scarce
Swallowtail, *Iphiclides podalirius*
(Europe & Asia), is shown in a
typical swallowtail resting
position, with its wings
folded above
its body.

Head

Thorax

Abdomen

**MAGNIFIED
SCALES**
A close-up view
of the eyespot of a
South American butterfly
reveals the
overlapping scales that
form the wing pattern. In
this picture, the tough
wing veins are
clearly visible.

*Rows of scales form the
beautiful patterns
and colours of butterfly
wings*

WHICH FAMILY?
The veins in the
wings of butterflies and moths
help to keep the wing in the
correct flight position. The
way the veins are arranged
also helps identify which
family of butterflies or
moths a species
belongs to.

COMING IN TO LAND
With its wings slightly
curved, a Peacock butterfly,
Inachis io (Europe), is about to
land on a buddleia. Butterflies
have such control over
their flight movements
that they can
make sudden
landings.

Temperate butterflies

"TEMPERATE" is how we describe the regions of the Earth with warm summers and cold winters. In these temperate areas butterflies are inactive during the winter months and so must be able to survive without feeding. Winter is often passed in the chrysalis stage, but there are a few butterflies in Europe and North America that pass the winter as adults, hibernating until the warmer spring weather (p. 51). The wide variety of flowers in temperate meadows and woodland clearings means that there are plenty of butterflies, although not as many as in the tropics (pp. 32-35). Temperate habitats have been increasingly destroyed and developed during recent years, and consequently butterflies are becoming less common. Their disappearance is especially sad because for most of us butterflies are the spirit of summer. Indeed, the term "butterfly" may well come from "butter-coloured fly", a name for the yellow-coloured Brimstone, which is one of the first European butterflies to appear each summer.

The Peacock, *Inachis io,* is one of the most common and distinctive butterflies in Europe and temperate Asia

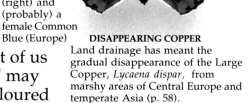

An old engraving of a Small Copper (right) and (probably) a female Common Blue (Europe)

DISAPPEARING COPPER
Land drainage has meant the gradual disappearance of the Large Copper, *Lycaena dispar,* from marshy areas of Central Europe and temperate Asia (p. 58).

Grassland butterflies

BEAUTIFUL BLUE
In Europe, the Adonis Blue, *Lysandra bellargus,* is threatened in areas where its grassland habitat is no longer grazed by rabbits or sheep. It is now protected by law in France.

BENEFITING EACH OTHER
Caterpillars of the Large Blue, *Maculinea arion* (Europe), live in ants' nests, where they feed on the ant larvae. The caterpillars are not attacked by the ants, who "milk" them for a sugary solution (p. 58).

GRASSLAND HABITAT
Species of butterfly whose caterpillars feed on grasses are found in meadows, heathlands and the edges of woodlands and rivers.

BROUGHT UP ON VIOLETS
The Aphrodite, *Speyeria aphrodite,* is found in the grasslands and open woodlands of western North America. The caterpillars feed on violets.

BROWN, OR BLACK AND WHITE?
Although belonging to the Satyridae family, or "browns", the Marbled White, *Melanargia galathea* (Europe & Asia), has a black-and-white pattern.

This butterfly probably gets its name because it enjoys basking on walls with its wings outspread

Sombre colours on the upper and underside provide good camouflage

SUCCESSFUL BROWN
The Meadow Brown, *Maniola jurtina* (Europe, Asia & Africa) is a typical well-camouflaged grassland butterfly.

SUN LOVER
The Wall butterfly, *Lasiommata megera* (Europe, Asia & N. Africa), is another grass-feeding species.

WIDESPREAD IN EUROPE
Although most coppers occur in Asia and America, the Purple-shot Copper, *Heodes alciphron,* is European.

A COMMON CRESCENTSPOT
The Field Crescentspot, *Phyciodes campestris,* is common in the uplands of western North America.

Woodland butterflies

Irregular dead-leaf outline and pattern gives effective camouflage

Oak leaves

GREEN CAMOUFLAGE
With its brown upperside and beautiful green underside, the Green Hairsteak, *Callophrys rubi* (Europe, Asia & N. Africa), has ideal woodland camouflage.

FROM COMMA TO HOP
The Comma, also popularly known as the Hop Merchant, *Polygonia comma*, is found in a wide range of woodlands in North America and Europe. It belongs to a group of butterflies called anglewings, in which different species have been named after their distinctive wing markings.

Upperside of Comma

The name "Comma" refers to a mark on the underside of the hind wing

Underside of Comma

Hairstreaks are usually dark on the upperside, with different colour variations on the underside

IN STREAMS TO CANYONS
The Acadian Hairstreak, *Satyrium acadica* (N. America), occurs in damp meadows, by streams, and in canyons.

OAK FOREST RESIDENT
The Purple Hairstreak, *Quercusia quercus*, is one of a number of European and Asian species of hairstreaks.

MIXED WOODLAND HABITAT
Because of the variety of food sources, more species of butterfly are found in mixed woodland than in any other habitat. Some species of butterfly can be found flying at a low level in shady woodland clearings, while others live high among the tree tops. Other species of butterfly live along woodland edges, and in areas where people have cleared forests.

Only males have shimmering wing scales that reflect purple when the light is at a particular angle

BROKEN PATTERN
The colour pattern of the Common Glider, *Neptis sappho* (Europe & Asia), is less noticeable in the dappled light of a woodland glade.

This is the form from southern Europe - the Speckled Wood in northern Europe has creamy-white markings

WOODLAND CAMOUFLAGE
The colour pattern of the Speckled Wood, *Pararge aegeria* (Europe, Asia & N. Africa), makes it especially difficult to spot in patches of sunlight.

FEEDS ON DEAD ANIMALS
Although the Purple Emperor, *Apatura iris* (Europe & Asia), flies high up in trees, the males are attracted to the ground to feed on rotting animal carcasses.

Pine White caterpillars sometimes completely strip pine trees of their leaves

INTO THE WOOD
The Woodland Grayling, *Hipparchia fagi* (Europe & Asia), blends with bark patterns on tree trunks.

PINE PEST
The adult Pine White, *Neophasia menapia* (N. America), lives among the pine trees on which its caterpillars feed.

FLYING TORTOISES
Large Tortoiseshells, *Nymphalis polychloros* (Europe & Asia), often occur in wooded uplands.

Mountain butterflies

Short antennae and long hairlike body scales of all *Parnassius* butterflies

Small Apollo, *Parnassius phoebus*, (Europe, Asia & N. America)

Of all the environments in which butterflies and moths live, the short summers, cold nights, and strong winds of the mountains and Arctic tundra are surely the most hostile. Insects have to adapt to survive harsh climates, which is why many mountain butterflies are darker than related species from lowland areas. Because darker colours absorb sunlight more easily, the insects can warm up rapidly in the early morning, when the air temperature is low. Other mountain and Arctic butterflies retain heat through the long, hairy scales that cover their bodies. The rocky terrain of high mountains causes many species to lay their eggs in rocky crevices rather than on plants, while the short summer season means that they can only breed once a year. Butterflies living in constant strong winds fly in low, short bursts to avoid being blown away, and many flatten themselves against rocks when at rest. Although few species are found at very high altitudes, there are notable exceptions of intrepid butterflies living on the very edge of the snow line in mountain ranges such as the Himalayas.

HIGH FLIER
The beautiful Apollo, *Parnassius apollo*, is found on some of the higher mountains of Europe and Asia. Because its many local forms are much sought after by collectors, it is now protected in most of Europe.

Male   Female

Although not a mountain species, the female Mottled Umber, Erannis defoliara, is wingless

FLIGHTLESS MOTHER
Some moths have wingless females, which can be an advantage on mountains where a moth could be blown away while laying its eggs.

Upperside of a Hermit butterfly

Underside of a Hermit butterfly

STONY SURVIVOR
One of the best ways for a butterfly to survive in a bare rocky environment is to be well camouflaged at all times. The Hermit butterfly, *Chazara briseis*, can be found on dry stony slopes in Central and southern Europe, and the Middle East.

HIGH MOUNTAIN HABITAT
Butterflies and moths are attracted to alpine meadows by the numerous summer flowers. This scene could be in the American Rockies, the European Alps, or the Asian Himalayas.

A species of Asian Pontia has been found at 4,250 m (14,000 feet) in northern India

CLOSE TO THE SNOW LINE
The Peak White butterfly, *Pontia callidice* (Europe & Asia), a relation of the Western White, *Pontia occidentalis* (N. America), is found near the snow line on high alpine mountains.

FRIEND OR ENEMY?
Found on higher ground in mainland Europe and Asia, the caterpillar of the Idas Blue, *Lycaeides idas*, spends the winter in ants' nests. The higher the altitude, the smaller this tiny butterfly becomes.

HIGH OR LOW
While Zephyr Blue, *Plebejus pylaon*, colonies are found in a variety of grassy habitats in Europe and Asia, the subspecies *trappi* occurs only in the central and southern European highlands.

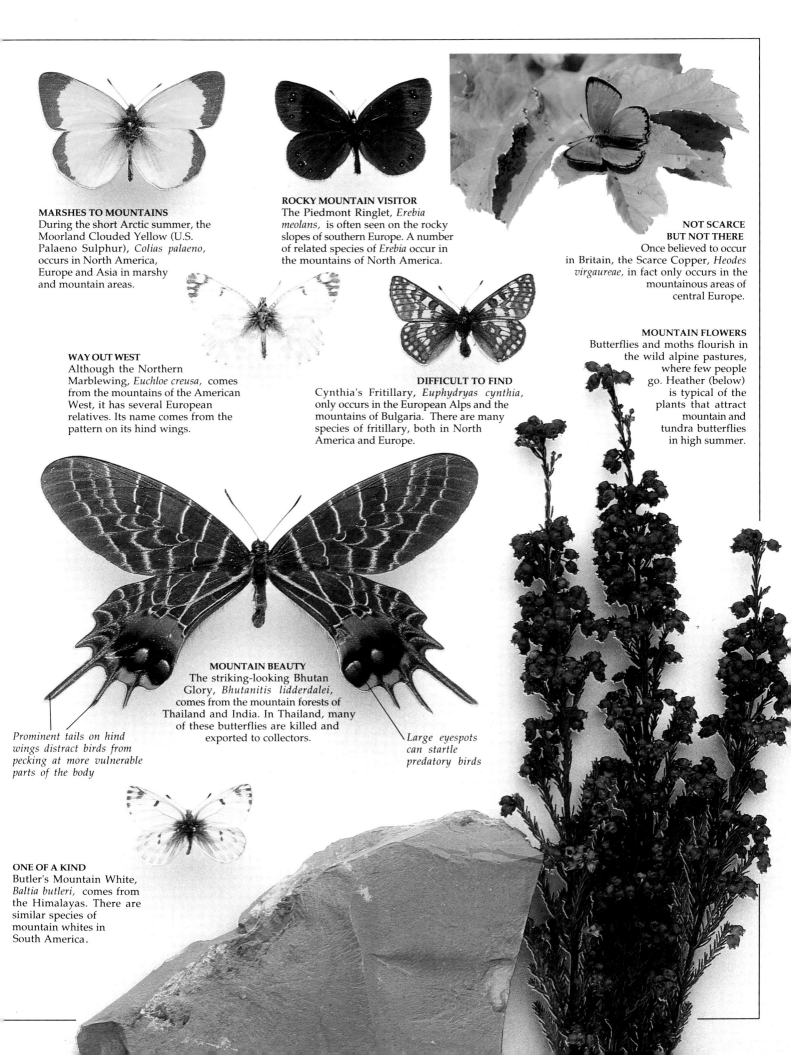

MARSHES TO MOUNTAINS
During the short Arctic summer, the Moorland Clouded Yellow (U.S. Palaeno Sulphur), *Colias palaeno*, occurs in North America, Europe and Asia in marshy and mountain areas.

ROCKY MOUNTAIN VISITOR
The Piedmont Ringlet, *Erebia meolans,* is often seen on the rocky slopes of southern Europe. A number of related species of *Erebia* occur in the mountains of North America.

NOT SCARCE BUT NOT THERE
Once believed to occur in Britain, the Scarce Copper, *Heodes virgaureae,* in fact only occurs in the mountainous areas of central Europe.

WAY OUT WEST
Although the Northern Marblewing, *Euchloe creusa,* comes from the mountains of the American West, it has several European relatives. Its name comes from the pattern on its hind wings.

DIFFICULT TO FIND
Cynthia's Fritillary, *Euphydryas cynthia,* only occurs in the European Alps and the mountains of Bulgaria. There are many species of fritillary, both in North America and Europe.

MOUNTAIN FLOWERS
Butterflies and moths flourish in the wild alpine pastures, where few people go. Heather (below) is typical of the plants that attract mountain and tundra butterflies in high summer.

MOUNTAIN BEAUTY
The striking-looking Bhutan Glory, *Bhutanitis lidderdalei,* comes from the mountain forests of Thailand and India. In Thailand, many of these butterflies are killed and exported to collectors.

Prominent tails on hind wings distract birds from pecking at more vulnerable parts of the body

Large eyespots can startle predatory birds

ONE OF A KIND
Butler's Mountain White, *Baltia butleri,* comes from the Himalayas. There are similar species of mountain whites in South America.

Exotic butterflies

No REGION has so many marvellously coloured and patterned butterflies as the tropics - the hot areas of the Earth that are near the Equator. The range of colour and pattern is quite remarkable, although we can only guess why some of these butterflies are so brightly coloured: it may be for display to attract a mate, but equally it may be a form of camouflage. In the bright tropical forest, with its deep shadows and intense patches of sunlight, a brightly coloured butterfly may not be conspicuous. In many species the bright colours warn predators that the butterflies are distasteful. But however wide a range of colour and pattern tropical butterflies display, they are less variable in shape than moths. There are also far fewer species of butterflies than moths in the world.

Trailing tails typical of many swallowtails

Unusual-shaped wings measure 127 mm (5 ins) across

FOREST MYSTERY *above*
Because it lives high up in the dense, steamy forests of New Guinea, it is hardly surprising that little is known about the Purple Spotted Swallowtail, *Graphium weiskei*.

BRILLIANT GREEN BEAUTY
Some of the most lovely butterflies are the large birdwing swallowtails of the New Guinea region. Species such as the *Ornithoptera priamus* are protected against over-trading, but not from the destruction of their habitat.

Males of priamus *group of birdwings have golden fringes on hind wings for transferring scent during courtship*

TROPICAL RAINFOREST HABITAT
Although tropical rainforests can be found in Southeast Asia, Northeast Australia, the South Pacific islands, and Central Africa, the place to look for the widest range of tropical butterflies is Central and South America. In these impenetrable areas, with no winter, abundant rainfall, and a huge variety of plants, butterflies have the perfect living quarters.

WET OR DRY *below*
When it flies, the highly visible Mother of Pearl, *Protogoniomorpha parhassus* (Africa), catches the light. But once at rest in the rainforest, its colour and shape make it look like a dead leaf. Mother of Pearls have wet and dry season forms: in the wet season the butterflies are smaller than in the dry season.

SPECTACULAR SWALLOWTAIL
The striking Cattle Heart Swallowtail, *Parides eurimedes*, is still quite common in parts of Central and South America. It can be seen from sea level to 1,500 m (5,000 ft), flying along the edges of rainforests.

Tail-less swallowtail

Irregularly shaped wing

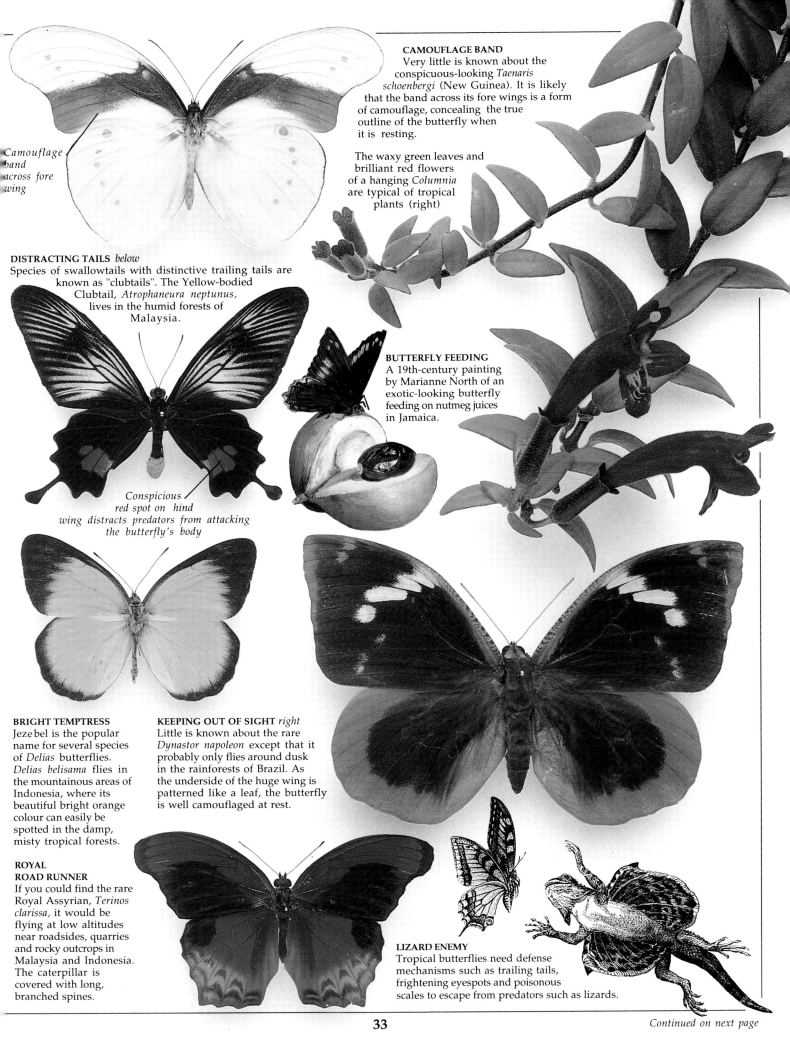

Camouflage band across fore wing

CAMOUFLAGE BAND
Very little is known about the conspicuous-looking *Taenaris schoenbergi* (New Guinea). It is likely that the band across its fore wings is a form of camouflage, concealing the true outline of the butterfly when it is resting.

The waxy green leaves and brilliant red flowers of a hanging *Columnia* are typical of tropical plants (right)

DISTRACTING TAILS *below*
Species of swallowtails with distinctive trailing tails are known as "clubtails". The Yellow-bodied Clubtail, *Atrophaneura neptunus*, lives in the humid forests of Malaysia.

Conspicious red spot on hind wing distracts predators from attacking the butterfly's body

BUTTERFLY FEEDING
A 19th-century painting by Marianne North of an exotic-looking butterfly feeding on nutmeg juices in Jamaica.

BRIGHT TEMPTRESS
Jezebel is the popular name for several species of *Delias* butterflies. *Delias belisama* flies in the mountainous areas of Indonesia, where its beautiful bright orange colour can easily be spotted in the damp, misty tropical forests.

KEEPING OUT OF SIGHT *right*
Little is known about the rare *Dynastor napoleon* except that it probably only flies around dusk in the rainforests of Brazil. As the underside of the huge wing is patterned like a leaf, the butterfly is well camouflaged at rest.

ROYAL ROAD RUNNER
If you could find the rare Royal Assyrian, *Terinos clarissa*, it would be flying at low altitudes near roadsides, quarries and rocky outcrops in Malaysia and Indonesia. The caterpillar is covered with long, branched spines.

LIZARD ENEMY
Tropical butterflies need defense mechanisms such as trailing tails, frightening eyespots and poisonous scales to escape from predators such as lizards.

33

Continued on next page

MORE COLOURFUL MALE
A collector brought this nymphlalid butterfly, *Myscelia orsis*, back from Paraguay many years ago. The vivid blue of this male contrasts sharply with the duller and more strongly patterned female.

NOT REALLY A MIMIC *right*
The male Danaid Eggfly looks quite different from the female (below). Other popular names for this species, found in Africa, N. & C. America, India & Australia, are the Mimic, Diadem, or Six-continents.

PART OF A GROUP *below*
The Theclid hairstreak, *Amblypodia morphina*, is one of a number of similar Southeast Asian butterflies.

Male butterfly

A female from this group of butterflies would be paler in colour than this male

Female butterfly

PERFECT LOOKALIKE *above*
The non-poisonous female Danaid Eggfly, *Hypolimnas misippus*, is a brilliant impersonator of the poisonous Tiger butterfly, *Danaus chrysippus* (mimicry pp. 56-57).

BRIGHT UNDERWINGS *right*
Like many butterflies, the underside (illustrated) of the Malay Lacewing, *Cethosia hypsaea* , has a more interesting pattern than the upperside. This specimen was collected in Borneo.

Butterfly's underside - upperside has plainer brown fore wing with broad white band

Bright red pattern typical of a poisonous butterfly's warning colours

An engraving of a tropical swallowtail, Papilio crino, (Sri Lanka)

Characteristic large wings of many swallowtails

POISONOUS GIANT
A wingspan of up to 250 mm (10 ins) makes the African Giant Swallowtail, *Papilio antimachus*, the largest African butterfly. The butterfly is believed to be extremely poisonous and is avoided by its enemies in the rainforest.

BEAT THIS CAMOUFLAGE *below*
Few butterflies have a more interesting resting camouflage than the South American butterfly *Coenophlebia archidona*.

Underside looks like a dead leaf

BANANA EATER *left*
The adults of *Taenaris macrops* (New Guinea) love feeding on ripe bananas. The caterpillars of some *Taenaris* butterflies feed on banana leaves.

Large eyespot for startling predators

Silvery patches imitate the fungi found on dead leaves

Broken pattern camouflage

MYSTERY MAP-WING
Although the Map-winged butterfly, *Cyrestis nivea*, is common in Malaysia and Indonesia, very little is known about its habits. Its broken pattern certainly gives it a formidable protective camouflage.

RAINFOREST DAZZLER
The group of South American butterflies called *Morphos* include some of the world's most dazzling butterflies (also pp. 24-25). The wings of species such as *Morpho cypris* are often used for jewellery.

ATTENTION SEEKER *below*
The easily recognizable Ruddy Daggerwing, *Marpesia petreus*, can be seen in woods and thickets in the southern United States, and Central and South America.

Long tails on hind wings distract would-be predators from attacking body, or the main part of the brightly coloured wings

Morpho butterflies are camouflaged by having brown underwings

Underside of male - the upperside is mostly white with a darker margin

"A COLLECTOR AT WORK"
In the 1920s, Arthur Twidle painted a number of scenes to illustrate his book *Beautiful Butterflies of the Tropics*.

MORPHO WING PENDANT
It is argued that the collection of millions of *Morpho* butterflies to use as jewellery does not affect the population as only males are collected. Female *Morphos* are not only less dazzling, but much shyer, making them difficult to catch in their rainforest habitats.

DULL ON TOP
Like other *Delias* butterflies, the Imperial White, *Delias harpalyce* (S. E. Australia) is unusual in having more brightly coloured undersides than upper.

This exotic lilly is called a Peace Lilly

Oblong collecting-box, lined at the top and bottom with cork

Method of setting a butterfly (below)

OWL'S HEAD
The huge South American Owl Butterflies get their name from the owl-like eyespots on the underside of the wings. Many birds will understandably keep away from anything resembling an owl. This species, *Caligo prometheus*, lives in the rain-forests of Ecuador and Colombia.

Eyespot on underside of Owl Butterfly's hind wings, shown on pp. 8-9

As they dislike bright sunshine, Owl butterflies fly in dark places, or at dusk

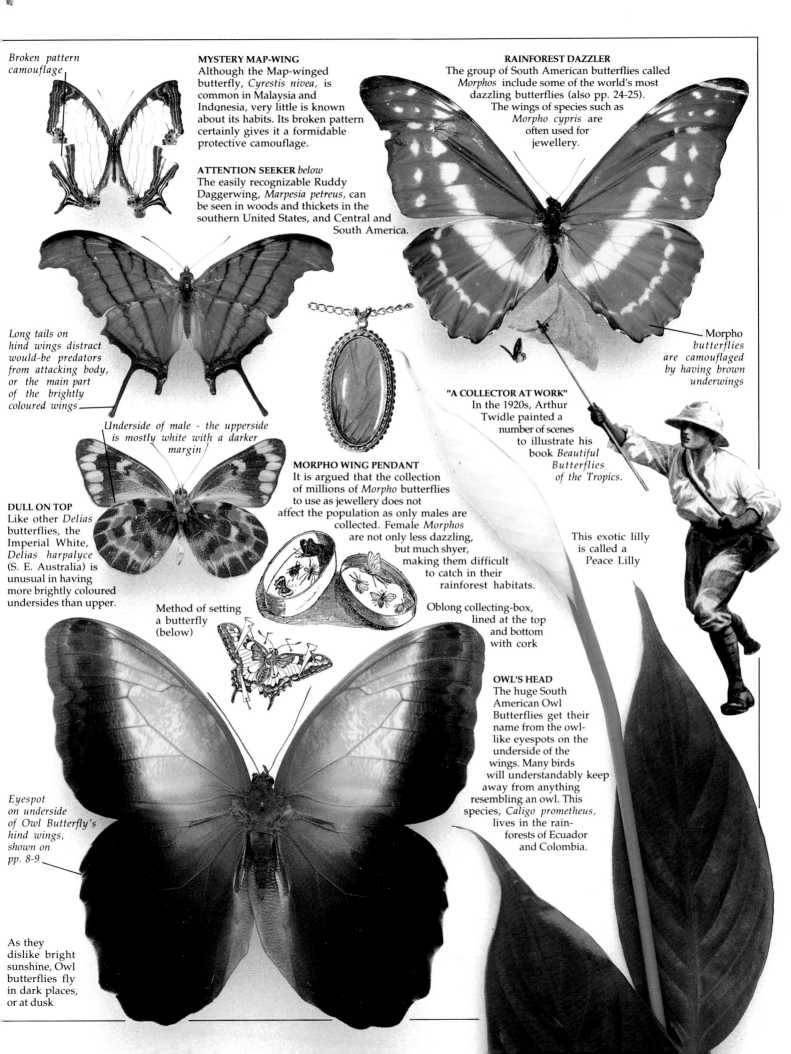

Moths

THERE ARE AT LEAST 150,000 DIFFERENT SPECIES of moths compared with some 15,000 butterflies. *Nachtschmetterlinge* ("night-butterflies"), the German word for moths, clearly reflects the popular view of their behaviour. While it is true that the majority of moths fly at dusk or during the night, quite a large number are day-flyers (pp. 48-49). Although moths such as the silkworm (pp. 40-41) are useful to people, a few species of moth are harmful. These include the moths that destroy crops, fruit, or trees; the clothes moths that damage woollen goods; and moths that spread diseases in cattle by feeding on the moisture around their eyes (p. 56). The majority of moths are harmless, pollinating flowers and forming a vital part of the complex web of life.

An engraving showing the main parts of a moth, with the darker lines representing the fascia, which are part of the wing pattern

THE LONGEST TONGUE?
This amazing proboscis belongs to Darwin's Hawk-moth, *Xanthopan morganii,* from Madagascar. Charles Darwin, the celebrated 19th-century English naturalist, knew of an orchid in which the nectar was at the base of a 30 cm (12 in) corolla. As the orchid obviously needed to be pollinated, Darwin thought there must be a moth with a proboscis between 30 and 35 cm (12 to 13 in). Years later, the discovery of this hawk-moth proved that Darwin's theory was correct.

Feeding

Like butterflies, most moths take nectar from flowers. You may be able to see day-flying moths (pp. 48-49) hovering in front of a flower as they feed. Many large moths do not feed at all as adults. During its short adult life, the Indian Moon Moth (right and below) lives entirely off food stored in its body during the caterpillar stage.

FINDING NECTAR *right*
The long proboscis of this hawk-moth seeks out nectar from flowers. During this probing, pollen is picked up and transferred from flower to flower.

Characteristic thick body and long fore wings of all hawk-moths. This group of moths are all powerful flyers

Head has the cerebral ganglion ("brain") inside. The eyes, antennae and sense organs called palps give the insect information about its environment

Antenna

Maxillary palp

3. Eye

Labial palp

Labial palp

Proboscis

FACE-TO-FACE WITH A MOTH
An almost head-on view of the Indian Moon Moth shows its antennae, and front and middle legs. The antennae have minute sense organs that probably detect not only scent but changes in air pressure.

As this moth does not feed as an adult it has no proboscis

This female Moon Moth uses its antennae to select the correct food plant on which to lay its eggs

Trailing tails help to protect this moth

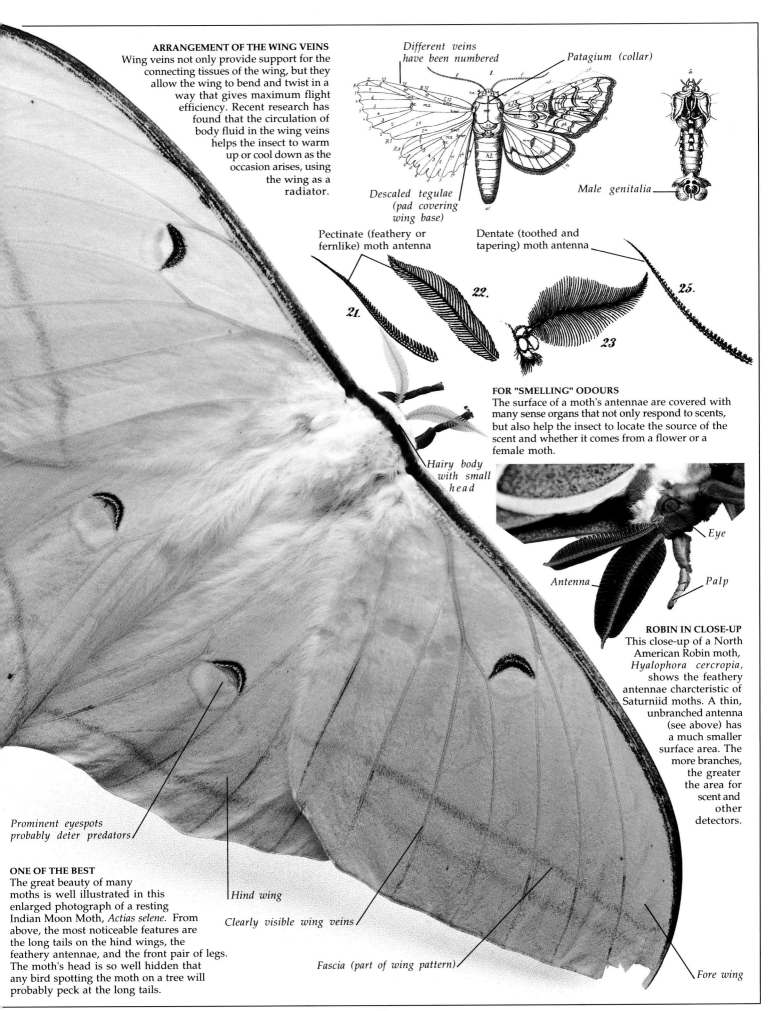

ARRANGEMENT OF THE WING VEINS

Wing veins not only provide support for the connecting tissues of the wing, but they allow the wing to bend and twist in a way that gives maximum flight efficiency. Recent research has found that the circulation of body fluid in the wing veins helps the insect to warm up or cool down as the occasion arises, using the wing as a radiator.

Different veins have been numbered

Patagium (collar)

Descaled tegulae (pad covering wing base)

Male genitalia

Pectinate (feathery or fernlike) moth antenna

Dentate (toothed and tapering) moth antenna

21.

22.

23.

25.

FOR "SMELLING" ODOURS

The surface of a moth's antennae are covered with many sense organs that not only respond to scents, but also help the insect to locate the source of the scent and whether it comes from a flower or a female moth.

Hairy body with small head

Eye

Antenna

Palp

ROBIN IN CLOSE-UP

This close-up of a North American Robin moth, *Hyalophora cercropia*, shows the feathery antennae charcteristic of Saturniid moths. A thin, unbranched antenna (see above) has a much smaller surface area. The more branches, the greater the area for scent and other detectors.

Prominent eyespots probably deter predators

ONE OF THE BEST

The great beauty of many moths is well illustrated in this enlarged photograph of a resting Indian Moon Moth, *Actias selene.* From above, the most noticeable features are the long tails on the hind wings, the feathery antennae, and the front pair of legs. The moth's head is so well hidden that any bird spotting the moth on a tree will probably peck at the long tails.

Hind wing

Clearly visible wing veins

Fascia (part of wing pattern)

Fore wing

Cocoons

Most moths spin a cocoon. This silken case encloses the caterpillar as it pupates and the inactive pupa while it is developing. Some species incorporate stinging hairs from the last caterpillar skin, or bits of plant material into the cocoon as added protection or camouflage. The development of cocoons reaches its peak in the silkmoths (pp. 40-41), whose cocoons are made up of a single thread (sometimes about 800 metres or half a mile long), wrapped round and round many times. When the adult moth is ready to emerge, it has to force its way out of the cocoon. This can be difficult, since the cocoon is often very hard. Some moths have a file-like organ with which to cut their way out; others produce a liquid that softens the walls. Many caterpillars also spin silken webs to protect themselves while they are feeding, although these are not true cocoons.

HANGING BY A THREAD
Some species suspend their cocoons from a long silken thread - an added protection against predatory insects.

IN DISGUISE
These silken moth cocoons look very much like a part of the plant from which they hang, safe from all but the most sharp-eyed predators.

"WOODEN" COCOON
This Green Silver-lines moth, *Bena fagana* (Europe), has just emerged. Its cocoon incorporated bits of bark chewed off by the caterpillar, to give strength and camouflage.

Large silken web extends across several leaves, giving the caterpillars plenty of room to move around and feed

Hard surface of cocoon, reinforced by fragments of bark

CATERPILLAR SHELTER
Silk is used extensively by caterpillars. Many species of *Yponomeuta* moths spin a protective web and live communally under it, feeding on the plant. Some of the smaller caterpillars may get blown around, and use the silk like a parachute.

Distinctive wing pattern shows how the Green Silver-lines gets its name

Flimsy net helps to keep pupa in place

UNDERGROUND NET
The pupae of the Silver-striped Hawk-moth, *Hippotion celerio* (Europe, Africa & Asia; also p. 19), have a very flimsy cocoon, consisting of a few strands of silk woven into a net.

BURIED ALIVE
Hawk-moths are one of the moth families that pupate below ground. The caterpillar makes a small cavity, and spins silk around the walls. This helps to protect it from the damp as well as from animals burrowing in the soil.

These moths pupate underground

Caterpillar that has fallen off the web hanging on its own thread of silk

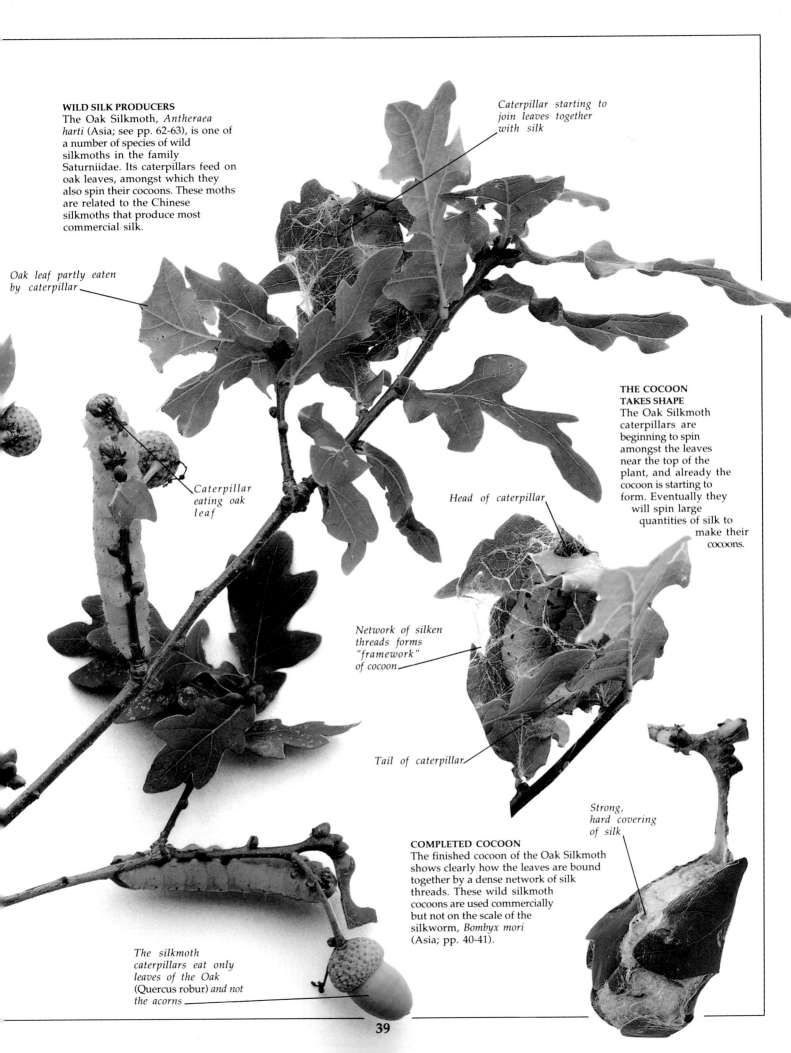

WILD SILK PRODUCERS
The Oak Silkmoth, *Antheraea harti* (Asia; see pp. 62-63), is one of a number of species of wild silkmoths in the family Saturniidae. Its caterpillars feed on oak leaves, amongst which they also spin their cocoons. These moths are related to the Chinese silkmoths that produce most commercial silk.

Oak leaf partly eaten by caterpillar

Caterpillar starting to join leaves together with silk

Caterpillar eating oak leaf

THE COCOON TAKES SHAPE
The Oak Silkmoth caterpillars are beginning to spin amongst the leaves near the top of the plant, and already the cocoon is starting to form. Eventually they will spin large quantities of silk to make their cocoons.

Head of caterpillar

Network of silken threads forms "framework" of cocoon

Tail of caterpillar

Strong, hard covering of silk

COMPLETED COCOON
The finished cocoon of the Oak Silkmoth shows clearly how the leaves are bound together by a dense network of silk threads. These wild silkmoth cocoons are used commercially but not on the scale of the silkworm, *Bombyx mori* (Asia; pp. 40-41).

The silkmoth caterpillars eat only leaves of the Oak (Quercus robur) and not the acorns

Silk moths

Illustrations from *Vermis sericus*, a popular 17th-century book on silkmoths

SILK IS PRODUCED by most moth caterpillars; but the finest quality silk is made by species of moths in the families Saturniidae and Bombycidae and, in particular, by the caterpillars of the large white moth, *Bombyx mori* (Asia), popularly known as the silkworm. According to Chinese legend, silk fibre was first discovered in about 2,700 B.C., but for centuries the methods used to produce silk commercially were kept a well-guarded secret - the export of silkworms or their eggs out of China was punishable by death. Eventually silkworm eggs, and the seeds of the mulberry trees the caterpillars feed on, were smuggled out of China, supposedly hidden in a walking stick.

Silk continued to command high prices in Europe - even after the Arabs had introduced silkworms into Spain, and silk weaving centres had been started in Italy. Nowadays the silkworm has become so domesticated that it no longer occurs in the wild.

SILKEN GOWNS
For many years, silk has been a highly prized material for luxurious wedding dresses and evening gowns.

REELING OF THE COCOONS
The 19th-century Chinese engraving shows the thread being transferred on to smaller bobbins. Today, silk-making is more mechanized, but the basic process remains the same.

UNWINDING THE THREAD
From its origins in China (above) to 17th-century Europe (below), the methods used to produce silk changed little. The insects inside the cocoons were killed in boiling water before they could hatch and break the thread of silk. The hot water also had the effect of dissolving the gum-like substance holding the strands together. The threads from several cocoons were then caught up, twisted together, and wound on a reel or frame.

3 BUILDING UP THE WALLS
The caterpillar has worked backwards and forwards between the leaves, making the cocoon thicker. All the time the silk is being forced out through the caterpillar's spinneret.

In ancient China, the cocoon shells were opened after the silk was removed, and the caterpillar eaten

Silk thread attached to surrounding leaves at many points

1 FINDING A SITE
The caterpillar of the silkworm, *Bombyx mori* (Asia), finds a suitable site surrounded by leaves before beginning to spin silk. This is produced by glands in the caterpillar's body and comes out through the spinneret under its head.

2 THE EARLY STAGES
To start with, the caterpillar spins a small web, weaving the silken thread into a loose cocoon. At this point, the network of the cocoon is not very dense, so the caterpillar is still clearly visible.

Almost-completed cocoon with dense walls of silk

Each cocoon is made of a single thread of silk which, when unravelled, is about 805 m (half a mile) long

4 INCREASING THE DENSITY
The thickness of the silk layer increases and the cocoon will now keep most parasites and predators away from the caterpillar.

5 A SAFE HAVEN
The cocoon is now strong enough to protect the caterpillar fully as it starts to pupate and, eventually, as it changes into a moth.

Fully protected caterpillar can now begin to pupate

Temperate moths

TEMPERATE MOTHS, like butterflies from the same regions (pp. 28-29), have to be able to survive the cold winter months. While some temperate moths remain at the egg stage, others pass the winter as caterpillars, perhaps concealed inside the stem of a plant. Many more survive as a pupa, which in some species is further protected in a cocoon (pp. 38-39). In the temperate areas of Europe, Asia and North America, a moth's life-cycle is synchronized with the spring and summer months when there are plenty of grasses and flowers. The greatest variety of temperate moths are found during warm summer nights, when they can be seen at windows, or flying around some other source of light. On a moonlit night it may just be possible to see them sipping the nectar from flowers. Although most temperate moths fly only by night, certain species are active in the daytime (pp. 48-49).

Female of species is white throughout; in the male, upper surface of hind wing is yellow

MISNAMED MOTH *above*
Despite its name, the Salt-marsh Moth, *Estigmene acrea*, occurs in a variety of habitats throughout North America and Mexico.

Featherlike antenna

Wings have faded after death - originally pale green colour

Adults do not feed

BEAUTIFUL SILK MOTH
The spectacular Luna Moth, *Actias luna*, is found only in North America. In recent years its numbers have decreased due to pollution and insecticides. Like the Indian Moon Moth (pp. 36-37), it is often bred in captivity.

Long tails on hind wings

Bright pattern warns predators that the moth is poisonous

POISONOUS TIGER *above*
Like other tiger moths, the Virgin Tiger Moth, *Grammia virgo* (N. America), is avoided by birds because of its distasteful body fluids.

HOLLOWING A HOME
The caterpillar of the Locust-bean moth, *Ectomyelois ceratoniae* (worldwide), pupates in hollowed-out thistle stems.

PALER TIGER MOTH *right*
This day-flying Zuni Tiger, *Arachnis zuni*, can be found in the southwestern United States and Mexico. Like the Virgin Tiger (above), it is warningly coloured.

Dull-coloured fore wings

When disturbed, the red hind wings are flashed to confuse predators

STARING EYES
The Eyed Hawk-moth, *Smerinthus ocellata* (Europe & Asia), gets its name from the eyespots on its hind wings. If the moth is disturbed, it moves its fore wings to reveal two large, staring eyes.

Eyespots scare enemies away

FRUIT EATER *left*
Because the caterpillar of the Codling moth, *Cydia pomonella* (worldwide), feeds on apples and pears, it is often called the apple maggot.

FLASHY HIND WINGS
Underwing moths are found in Europe, Asia and America. The Bronze underwing, *Catocala cara*, is a North American species, whose range covers Canada to Florida.

PINES ARE FINE
By feeding on pine trees, the caterpillar of the Resin-gall moth, *Petrova resinella* (Europe, N. America & Asia), causes lumps of resin to be released.

ELEPHANT, HAWK, OR MOTH?
The attractive Elephant Hawk-moth, *Deilephila elpenor* (Europe & Asia), gets its name from the trunklike shape of the caterpillar.

Moth can be seen at dusk hovering in front of flowers from which it feeds

LOOPING ALONG *left*
The caterpillar of the Swallow-tail Moth, *Ourapteryx sambucaria* (Europe & Asia), moves its body by a series of "looping" actions. In the United States similar caterpillars are called inchworms, or measuring worms.

Skull and crossbones

Large hairy body

LIKE A BROKEN TWIG
The Buff-tip, *Phalera bucephala* (Europe & Asia), manages to look exactly like a twig when it is at rest. The yellow areas on the end of its wings and around its head explain why it is so named.

Wing pattern blends well into a tree

SKULL-LIKE MARKINGS
One of the most interesting moths is the Death's-head Hawk-moth, *Acherontia atropos* (Europe, Asia & Africa). Not only does it have a skull-like pattern on its body, but it also squeaks if disturbed. The caterpillar feeds on the leaves of the potato plant. The adult sometimes steals honey from beehives (also pp. 14-15).

BIG IN EUROPE
The largest European moth, the Great Peacock Moth, or Viennese Emperor, *Saturnia pyri*, belongs to the same family as the giant silk moths. It can be found mostly in southern Europe and western Asia.

Beautiful bright green colour has faded after death

FADED BEAUTY
The Large Emerald, *Geometra papilionaria* (Europe & Asia), has looper or inchworm caterpillars that hibernate on twigs.

COMPARE THE HIND WINGS
Closely related to the Bronze underwing (opposite page), the Clifden Nonpareil, *Catocala fraxini*, is found throughout Europe and Asia. Its beautiful hind wings have a quite different pattern to its duller fore wings.

Eyespots for startling predators

Wing span up to 70 mm (nearly 3 in)

A DRINKING HABIT
Philudoria potatoria is known as the Drinker because of the caterpillar's habit of drinking dew off the grasses on which it feeds. It is found in damp places throughout Europe, and in Asia as far as Japan.

Strongly patterned hind wing

Beautiful reddish-brown colouring provides good camouflage when at rest

Exotic moths

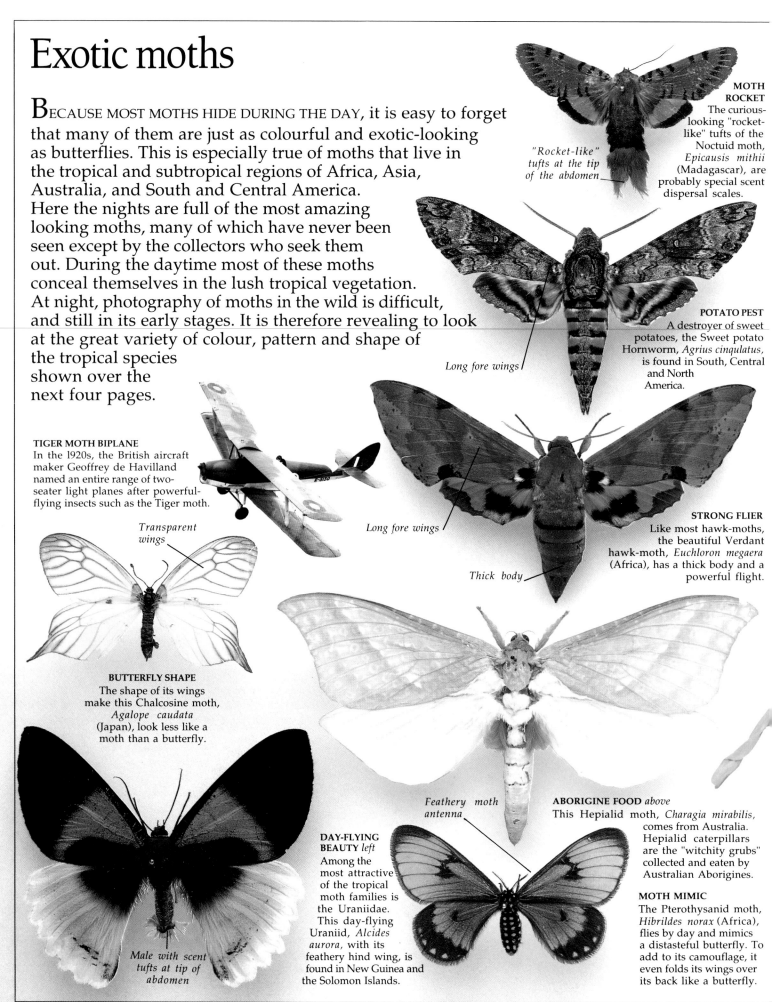

BECAUSE MOST MOTHS HIDE DURING THE DAY, it is easy to forget that many of them are just as colourful and exotic-looking as butterflies. This is especially true of moths that live in the tropical and subtropical regions of Africa, Asia, Australia, and South and Central America. Here the nights are full of the most amazing looking moths, many of which have never been seen except by the collectors who seek them out. During the daytime most of these moths conceal themselves in the lush tropical vegetation. At night, photography of moths in the wild is difficult, and still in its early stages. It is therefore revealing to look at the great variety of colour, pattern and shape of the tropical species shown over the next four pages.

MOTH ROCKET
The curious-looking "rocket-like" tufts of the Noctuid moth, *Epicausis mithii* (Madagascar), are probably special scent dispersal scales.

"Rocket-like" tufts at the tip of the abdomen

POTATO PEST
A destroyer of sweet potatoes, the Sweet potato Hornworm, *Agrius cinqulatus*, is found in South, Central and North America.

Long fore wings

TIGER MOTH BIPLANE
In the l920s, the British aircraft maker Geoffrey de Havilland named an entire range of two-seater light planes after powerful-flying insects such as the Tiger moth.

Transparent wings

Long fore wings

STRONG FLIER
Like most hawk-moths, the beautiful Verdant hawk-moth, *Euchloron megaera* (Africa), has a thick body and a powerful flight.

Thick body

BUTTERFLY SHAPE
The shape of its wings make this Chalcosine moth, *Agalope caudata* (Japan), look less like a moth than a butterfly.

Feathery moth antenna

ABORIGINE FOOD *above*
This Hepialid moth, *Charagia mirabilis*, comes from Australia. Hepialid caterpillars are the "witchity grubs" collected and eaten by Australian Aborigines.

DAY-FLYING BEAUTY *left*
Among the most attractive of the tropical moth families is the Uraniidae. This day-flying Uraniid, *Alcides aurora*, with its feathery hind wing, is found in New Guinea and the Solomon Islands.

MOTH MIMIC
The Pterothysanid moth, *Hibrildes norax* (Africa), flies by day and mimics a distasteful butterfly. To add to its camouflage, it even folds its wings over its back like a butterfly.

Male with scent tufts at tip of abdomen

TRAILING TAILS *below*
One of the strikingly beautiful Saturniidae family, the Madagascan Moon Moth, *Argema mittrei*, has large startling eyespots on its wings.

EAST AND WEST *right*
In this old engraving, two South American hawk-moths, of the species *Xylopanes chiron*, are seen with an Asian moth, *Euchromia polymena* (top).

Males usually have strongly feathered antennae

Thorax densely covered with hair

Trailing hind wing comes away if moth is attacked by predator

Delicately fringed tail

MULTICOLOURED BRILLIANCE *right*
Not surprisingly, the beautiful Jamaican Uraniid moth, *Urania sloanus*, is often mistaken for a butterfly. A closer look reveals the long slender moth antennae.

FLASHY TYPE
Like other Castniid moths, *Cyanostola hoppi* (C. America) is a day-flyer with bright "flash" colours on its hind wings. When the resting moth moves its wings, the sudden flash of colour scares away would-be predators.

Startling colour on hind wings

Fern-like antenna

SHAPE BREAKER
When resting, this Noctuid moth from South America holds its hind wings slightly in front of its fore wings. This will confuse predators by breaking up the moth's shape. The tufts or long scales are hair pencils (pp. 56-57) for the male moth to disperse its scent.

BIG MOTH, SMALL FAMILY
The Brahmaeidae are one of the smallest moth families, with only about 20 known species. This Brahmaeid moth, *Brahmaea wallichii*, with its wonderful swirling camouflage pattern, comes from Southeast Asia.

Striking camouflage pattern includes startling eyespot

45

Continued on next page

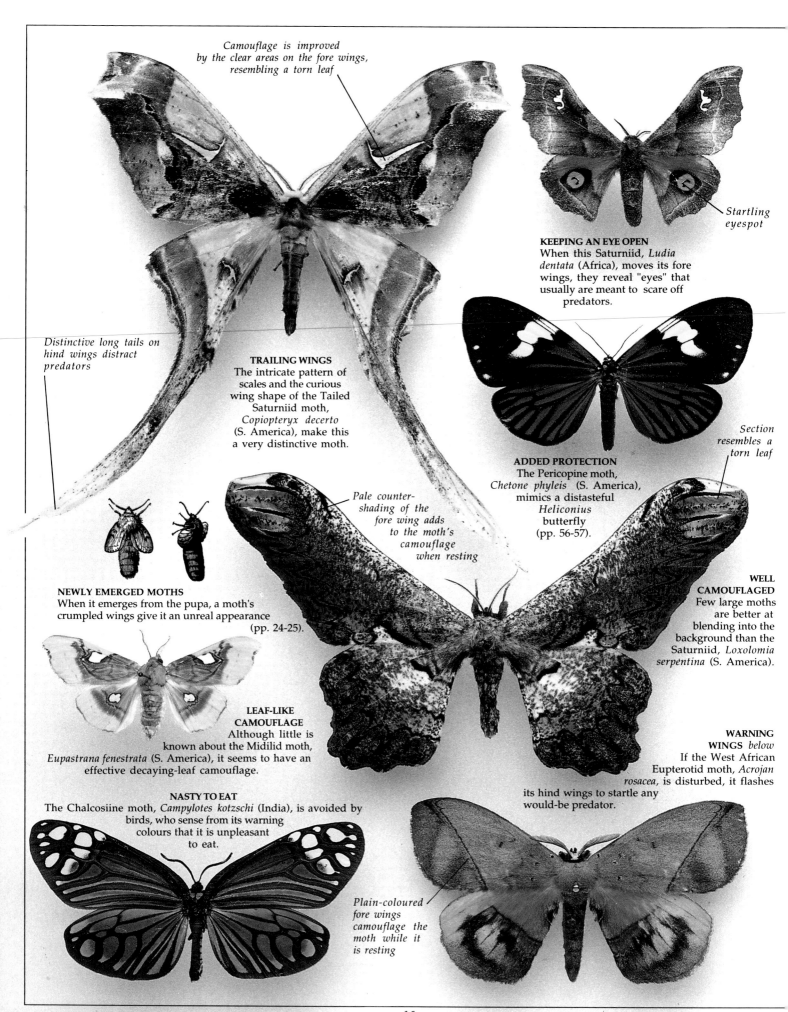

*Camouflage is improved
by the clear areas on the fore wings,
resembling a torn leaf*

*Startling
eyespot*

KEEPING AN EYE OPEN
When this Saturniid, *Ludia
dentata* (Africa), moves its fore
wings, they reveal "eyes" that
usually are meant to scare off
predators.

*Distinctive long tails on
hind wings distract
predators*

TRAILING WINGS
The intricate pattern of
scales and the curious
wing shape of the Tailed
Saturniid moth,
Copiopteryx decerto
(S. America), make this
a very distinctive moth.

*Section
resembles a
torn leaf*

ADDED PROTECTION
The Pericopine moth,
Chetone phyleis (S. America),
mimics a distasteful
Heliconius
butterfly
(pp. 56-57).

*Pale counter-
shading of the
fore wing adds
to the moth's
camouflage
when resting*

**WELL
CAMOUFLAGED**
Few large moths
are better at
blending into the
background than the
Saturniid, *Loxolomia
serpentina* (S. America).

NEWLY EMERGED MOTHS
When it emerges from the pupa, a moth's
crumpled wings give it an unreal appearance
(pp. 24-25).

**LEAF-LIKE
CAMOUFLAGE**
Although little is
known about the Midilid moth,
Eupastrana fenestrata (S. America), it seems to have an
effective decaying-leaf camouflage.

**WARNING
WINGS** *below*
If the West African
Eupterotid moth, *Acrojan
rosacea*, is disturbed, it flashes
its hind wings to startle any
would-be predator.

NASTY TO EAT
The Chalcosiine moth, *Campylotes kotzschi* (India), is avoided by
birds, who sense from its warning
colours that it is unpleasant
to eat.

*Plain-coloured
fore wings
camouflage the
moth while it
is resting*

DIVIDED WINGS *above*
The unusual Many-plume moth, *Orneodes dohertyi* (Africa), has its fore and hind wings divided into six parts.

Each wing segment fringed with scales

The temperate adult Emperor Moth, *Saturnia pavonia* (Europe), has the same fernlike antennae as the related tropical Atlas moth (below)

CAREFUL TASTER *above*
The Chrysaugine, *Arbina penicillana* (S. America), is one of a group of pyralid moths, which for unknown reasons, have very long labial palps (sense organs).

Long labial palp may be for examining food

Fore wing measures 200 mm (8 inches) from tip to tip

DAY-FLIER
The strikingly patterned Agaristine moth, *Longicella mollis*, is a day-flier from Indonesia.

Male has fernlike antennae for detecting the scent of females, characteristic of Saturniid moths

Shiny unscaled area that may confuse predators by reflecting light like a mirror

MONSTER MOTH
Atlas moths, such as this *Archaeoattacus edwardsi* (India), are among the largest moths in the world; certainly their wing area is greater than any other species of moth.

FLASHY MOVER *below*
Some species of day-flying Zygaenid moths (Southeast Asia) have a metallic sheen to their wings that changes with different angles of light. This moth is *Erasmia pulchella*.

MOTH OR WASP? *below*
Because the curious pattern and long antennae of this Agaristine moth, *Cocytius durvilli* (New Guinea), resemble a bee or wasp in flight, it is left alone by would-be predators.

Bright colours warn predators that the moth is distasteful to eat

Transparent wings help to make the moth look like a wasp

47

Day-flying moths

Moths are usually thought to be creatures of the night. While this is true of the majority of the 150,000 species, there are a large number that are day-flyers. Many moths will fly by day if disturbed, but the ones illustrated on these two pages are specialist day-flyers. Flying during the day means that in many ways they behave like butterflies, but the structure of their bodies, particularly the way in which their front and hind wings link together, shows that they are moths. Many of them can be seen around flowers, and are often mistaken for butterflies. But their wing shapes are usually different and their antennae do not generally end in a club (pp. 6-7). There are, however, always exceptions: the Zygaenid moths have swollen antennae, and species of Urania moths have butterfly-shaped wings, although their antennae are slender and moth-like. Some of these insects belong to families in which the majority are night-fliers while others, like the Zygaenidae, are mainly day-flying moths. Day-flyers include many interesting species such as the Hummingbird Hawk-moth, which hovers in front of flowers, sucking out nectar with its long proboscis. Many day-flying moths are also brightly coloured and conspicuous.

These two Pyralids are (top) the Gold Spot, *Pyraustra purpuralis* (Europe & Asia), and the Small Magpie, *Eurrhypara hortulata*, (Europe & Asia).

STRIPED BODY
The wings of this Euchromiid, *Euchromia lethe* (Africa), are not as decorative as those of some moths, but it has brightly coloured bands across its body. Many moths have striped bodies. Some mimic wasps, while others are even more vividly coloured. This species is sometimes found on imported bananas.

"Furry" bee-like striped abdomen

ROOT BORER
The Big-root Borer, or Bee Moth, *Melittia gloriosa* (N. America), bears a striking similarity to a bee. This is even more obvious from its flight and its behaviour in the field. This species feeds on the roots of squashes and gourds.

Butterfly-shaped wings and slender antennae, together with its bright colours, make this a particularly striking moth

SWEET TEMPTATIONS
To encourage butterflies and moths to come to your garden you should grow plants that attract them with nectar and perfume. Some plants, like species of Hebe (right), Buddleia and Aster, are particularly attractive to butterflies and moths.

POISON EATER
Sloan's Uraniid Moth, *Urania sloanus* (Jamaica), has unusual feeding habits. The caterpillars feed on species of plants that are poisonous to most animals but not to this insect, which derives protection from the poison.

SLOW FLYER
This Pericopine, *Gnophaela arizonae* (N. & C. America), is a slow-flying moth often found in great numbers in meadows over 2,500 m (8,200 ft) above sea-level. Its slow flight, bold pattern and daytime activity suggest that predators avoid it because it is distasteful.

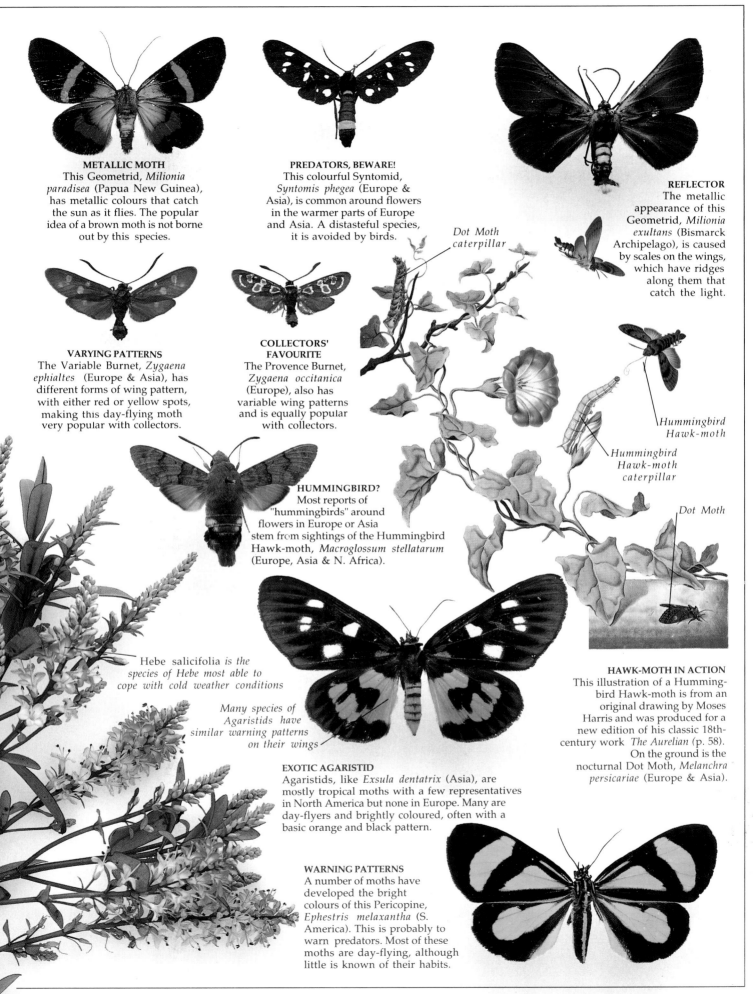

METALLIC MOTH
This Geometrid, *Milionia paradisea* (Papua New Guinea), has metallic colours that catch the sun as it flies. The popular idea of a brown moth is not borne out by this species.

PREDATORS, BEWARE!
This colourful Syntomid, *Syntomis phegea* (Europe & Asia), is common around flowers in the warmer parts of Europe and Asia. A distasteful species, it is avoided by birds.

REFLECTOR
The metallic appearance of this Geometrid, *Milionia exultans* (Bismarck Archipelago), is caused by scales on the wings, which have ridges along them that catch the light.

Dot Moth caterpillar

VARYING PATTERNS
The Variable Burnet, *Zygaena ephialtes* (Europe & Asia), has different forms of wing pattern, with either red or yellow spots, making this day-flying moth very popular with collectors.

COLLECTORS' FAVOURITE
The Provence Burnet, *Zygaena occitanica* (Europe), also has variable wing patterns and is equally popular with collectors.

Hummingbird Hawk-moth

Hummingbird Hawk-moth caterpillar

HUMMINGBIRD?
Most reports of "hummingbirds" around flowers in Europe or Asia stem from sightings of the Hummingbird Hawk-moth, *Macroglossum stellatarum* (Europe, Asia & N. Africa).

Dot Moth

Hebe salicifolia is the species of Hebe most able to cope with cold weather conditions

Many species of Agaristids have similar warning patterns on their wings

HAWK-MOTH IN ACTION
This illustration of a Humming-bird Hawk-moth is from an original drawing by Moses Harris and was produced for a new edition of his classic 18th-century work *The Aurelian* (p. 58). On the ground is the nocturnal Dot Moth, *Melanchra persicariae* (Europe & Asia).

EXOTIC AGARISTID
Agaristids, like *Exsula dentatrix* (Asia), are mostly tropical moths with a few representatives in North America but none in Europe. Many are day-flyers and brightly coloured, often with a basic orange and black pattern.

WARNING PATTERNS
A number of moths have developed the bright colours of this Pericopine, *Ephestris melaxantha* (S. America). This is probably to warn predators. Most of these moths are day-flying, although little is known of their habits.

Migration and hibernation

Bird MIGRATION HAS BEEN KNOWN about for hundreds if not thousands of years, but the migration of butterflies and moths is a relatively recent discovery. Unlike birds, most butterflies migrate in one direction only - from the place where they were born to a new area. There are several possible reasons for this - to avoid overpopulation; to find a new home when a temporary habitat such as agricultural land is destroyed; or to respond to the changing seasons. While birds tend to migrate at the onset of bad weather, butterflies and moths often migrate when the weather improves. For example, some species move north from North Africa and southern Europe as new plant growth becomes available for egg laying. It may not be a direct flight - they may breed on the way.

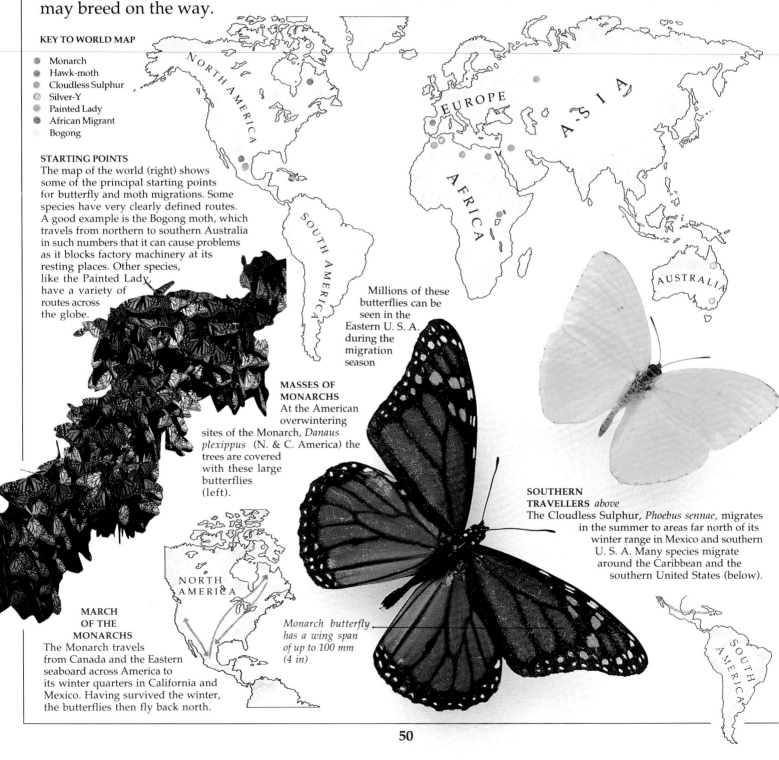

KEY TO WORLD MAP

- Monarch
- Hawk-moth
- Cloudless Sulphur
- Silver-Y
- Painted Lady
- African Migrant
- Bogong

STARTING POINTS
The map of the world (right) shows some of the principal starting points for butterfly and moth migrations. Some species have very clearly defined routes. A good example is the Bogong moth, which travels from northern to southern Australia in such numbers that it can cause problems as it blocks factory machinery at its resting places. Other species, like the Painted Lady, have a variety of routes across the globe.

Millions of these butterflies can be seen in the Eastern U. S. A. during the migration season

MASSES OF MONARCHS
At the American overwintering sites of the Monarch, *Danaus plexippus* (N. & C. America) the trees are covered with these large butterflies (left).

SOUTHERN TRAVELLERS *above*
The Cloudless Sulphur, *Phoebus sennae*, migrates in the summer to areas far north of its winter range in Mexico and southern U. S. A. Many species migrate around the Caribbean and the southern United States (below).

MARCH OF THE MONARCHS
The Monarch travels from Canada and the Eastern seaboard across America to its winter quarters in California and Mexico. Having survived the winter, the butterflies then fly back north.

Monarch butterfly has a wing span of up to 100 mm (4 in)

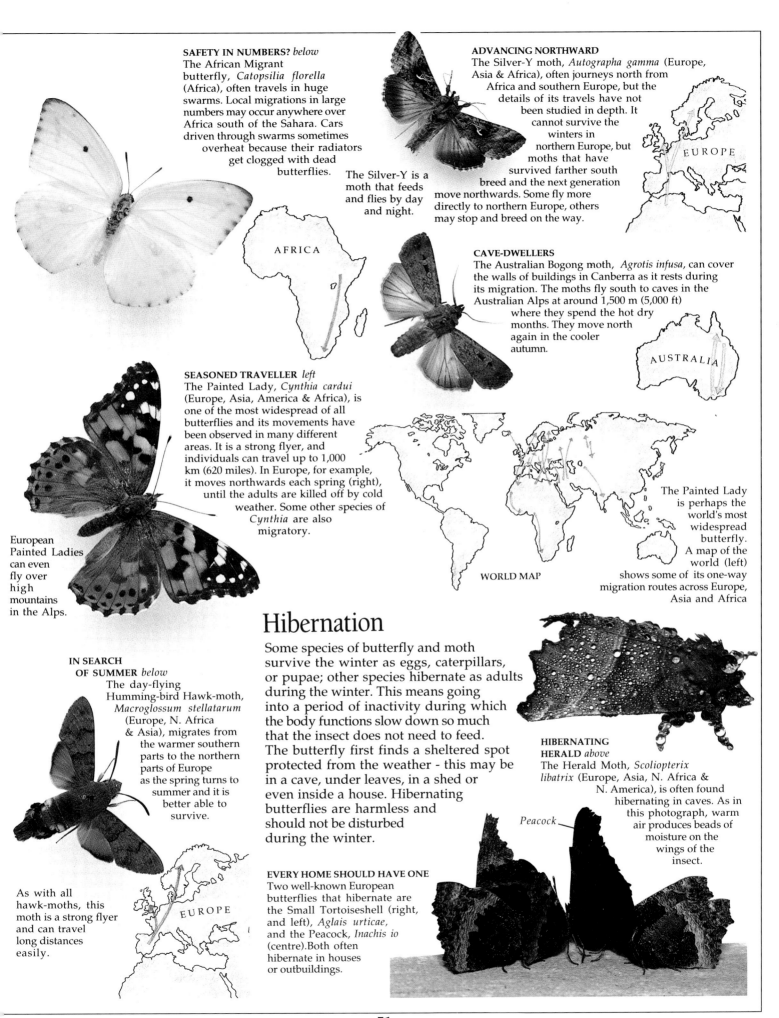

SAFETY IN NUMBERS? *below*
The African Migrant butterfly, *Catopsilia florella* (Africa), often travels in huge swarms. Local migrations in large numbers may occur anywhere over Africa south of the Sahara. Cars driven through swarms sometimes overheat because their radiators get clogged with dead butterflies.

The Silver-Y is a moth that feeds and flies by day and night.

ADVANCING NORTHWARD
The Silver-Y moth, *Autographa gamma* (Europe, Asia & Africa), often journeys north from Africa and southern Europe, but the details of its travels have not been studied in depth. It cannot survive the winters in northern Europe, but moths that have survived farther south breed and the next generation move northwards. Some fly more directly to northern Europe, others may stop and breed on the way.

EUROPE

AFRICA

CAVE-DWELLERS
The Australian Bogong moth, *Agrotis infusa*, can cover the walls of buildings in Canberra as it rests during its migration. The moths fly south to caves in the Australian Alps at around 1,500 m (5,000 ft) where they spend the hot dry months. They move north again in the cooler autumn.

AUSTRALIA

SEASONED TRAVELLER *left*
The Painted Lady, *Cynthia cardui* (Europe, Asia, America & Africa), is one of the most widespread of all butterflies and its movements have been observed in many different areas. It is a strong flyer, and individuals can travel up to 1,000 km (620 miles). In Europe, for example, it moves northwards each spring (right), until the adults are killed off by cold weather. Some other species of *Cynthia* are also migratory.

European Painted Ladies can even fly over high mountains in the Alps.

WORLD MAP

The Painted Lady is perhaps the world's most widespread butterfly. A map of the world (left) shows some of its one-way migration routes across Europe, Asia and Africa.

Hibernation

Some species of butterfly and moth survive the winter as eggs, caterpillars, or pupae; other species hibernate as adults during the winter. This means going into a period of inactivity during which the body functions slow down so much that the insect does not need to feed. The butterfly first finds a sheltered spot protected from the weather - this may be in a cave, under leaves, in a shed or even inside a house. Hibernating butterflies are harmless and should not be disturbed during the winter.

HIBERNATING HERALD *above*
The Herald Moth, *Scoliopterix libatrix* (Europe, Asia, N. Africa & N. America), is often found hibernating in caves. As in this photograph, warm air produces beads of moisture on the wings of the insect.

IN SEARCH OF SUMMER *below*
The day-flying Humming-bird Hawk-moth, *Macroglossum stellatarum* (Europe, N. Africa & Asia), migrates from the warmer southern parts to the northern parts of Europe as the spring turns to summer and it is better able to survive.

As with all hawk-moths, this moth is a strong flyer and can travel long distances easily.

EUROPE

EVERY HOME SHOULD HAVE ONE
Two well-known European butterflies that hibernate are the Small Tortoiseshell (right, and left), *Aglais urticae*, and the Peacock, *Inachis io* (centre). Both often hibernate in houses or outbuildings.

Peacock

Shape, colour and pattern

MOTHS ARE AMONG the most colourful creatures in the world. Butterflies have been described as "flying flowers", but moths have unrivalled wing patterns, as well as showing more variation in the shape of their wings. Colour and pattern play important roles in the lives of these insects. They may provide protection by means of camouflage (pp. 50-51), or they may help to advertise a moth's presence. By making the insect conspicuous, the colours may remind predators that the creature is distasteful and should be avoided; bright colours may also be imitative of a dangerous insect such as a wasp - another way of deterring predators. On the other hand, striking colours may also help to attract a mate.

MOTH OR WASP?
The day-flying Hornet Clearwing Moth, *Sesia apiformis* (America, Europe & Asia), looks like a hornet and even has a similar flight pattern. Few predators would be rash enough to risk attacking this insect.

SHARP DRESSER
The Noctuid *Apsara radians* (Asia) has a thorn-like wing pattern.

VANISHING OUTLINE
Markings disguise the shape of the African Noctuid *Mazuca strigicincta*.

DISAPPEARING TRICK
The Noctuid *Diphthera festiva* (C. & S. America) is almost invisible against a suitable background.

DELICATE PATTERNS
This Noctuid, *Baorisa hieroglyphica* (E. Asia), has lines and stripes that break up its wings.

PUTTING OFF BIRDS
The caterpillar of the Alder Moth, *Acronicta alni* (Europe), looks like a bird dropping when it is small. In its later stages it takes on a more aggressive appearance as the white markings are replaced by orange. Hairs along its back give it its unusual shape.

Wing pattern acts as camouflage

False "eyes"

Flagella

FEARSOME FOE
The caterpillar of the Puss Moth, *Cerura vinula* (Europe & Asia), uses red markings and false "eyes" in its aggression display. It also waves the thread-like extensions (flagella) on its tail.

EYES IN THE DARK
Shape and pattern combine to make this Sematurid moth, *Nothus lunus* (C. & S. America), inconspicuous at rest. The eyespots on the tail may be used to deter predators, although this has not yet been observed in the wild.

Eyespot

PEARL OF THE ORIENT
This Pyralid moth, *Margaronia quadrimaculalis* (E. Asia), has pearl-like white wings, broken up by a brown pattern.

MOTH IN WASP'S CLOTHING
This Pyralid, *Glyphodes militans* (E. Asia), gains some protection because its body looks like a wasp's.

THE LARGEST MOTH *below*
Being so large presents problems of defence for the Ghost Moth, *Thysania agrippina* (C. & S. America). For protection, it uses its delicate wing pattern as camouflage against tree trunks.

SPOTTED WINGS
The fore wings of the Thyridid *Rhodononeura limatula* (Madagascar) provide effective camouflage.

BIRD DECOY
The Uraniid moth *Micronia astheniata* (Asia) has lines that break up its pale-coloured wings. The tail spots may attract birds to peck the wings rather than the delicate body.

CONFUSION OF COLOURS
Cerace xanthocosma (Japan), with its spots and swirls of colour, is aptly named the Kaleidoscope Moth.

RED FOR DANGER
The Arctiid *Composia credula* (W. Indies) has a pattern of red and black, warning predators that it is distasteful.

Wing span up to 300 mm (12 in)

Tail goes up to indicate aggression

A CROSS LOBSTER
The caterpillar of the Lobster Moth, *Stauropus fagi* (Europe & Asia), looks like a lobster when in a defensive posture. The head goes up and back, while the tail is held up and forward. Like the Puss Moth caterpillar, it also waves its tail.

WAVY LINES
In the Tortricid *Acleris emargana* (N. America, Europe & Asia) the principle of camouflage is to avoid straight lines in its pattern - the fore wing is particularly wavy. The fore wings conceal the white hind wings at rest and the moth "vanishes" against its background .

Wavy fore wing

"LONG-TAILED" MOTH
Himantopterus marshalii, a Zygaenid moth from Africa, is given its distinctive shape by long hind wings that look like tails. The moth flutters above the grass with the hind wings floating up and down behind.

Distinctive hind wing like long tails

Camouflage

ALL WILD CREATURES have ways of protecting themselves from their enemies. For edible butterflies and moths a successful way of avoiding an early death is to "disappear" into their surroundings. They may do this by mimicking another object, or they may take on the patterns and colours of local trees, rocks, or leaves. Because they are especially vulnerable in daylight hours, many caterpillars and resting moths have perfected the art of concealment. Butterflies, which are active by day, and which usually rest with their wings together over their backs, have adopted other forms of camouflage. Some forest butterflies rest like moths with their wings spread out, while other species disguise themselves as either living or decaying leaves. The butterfly that has perfected this clever form of camouflage is the Indian Leaf butterfly, truly a master of disguise.

DEADLY ENEMY *left*
One of the main reasons why many moths and butterflies camouflage themselves is to escape from predatory birds.

Butterfly's upright head

Butterfly's wing

Leaf butterfly at rest on stem

Brown underside of Leaf butterfly

Orange-and-blue upperside of Leaf butterfly

INDIAN LEAF-TRICK
The most dramatic example of butterfly camouflage is the Indian Leaf butterfly, *Kallima inachus* (S.E. Asia). At rest, the butterfly has a remarkably close resemblance to a decaying leaf on a stem. It frequently rests on the ground in leaf-litter, where it becomes virtually invisible.

Resemblance to stalk and veins of a leaf

WRONG PECKING ORDER *left*
The tiny spots on the tail of this Uraniid moth, *Cyphura pardata* (New Guinea), may well distract birds, which might otherwise peck at more vital parts of its body. The moth can then escape, even if its wing is slightly torn. The main part of the wings shows a disruptive pattern when the insect is at rest.

Disruptive wing pattern

CITY MOTH, COUNTRY MOTH *right*
Some years ago, it was realized that the city form of the Peppered moth, *Biston betularia* (Europe), had gradually changed from a light to a black colour. This was to escape birds, which could easily spot a light-coloured moth on a smoke-polluted tree. In the countryside the same moth is still speckled white.

Black form

Speckled form

NOT LIKE A MOTH *right*
These Noctuid moths, photographed in a Costa Rican rain-forest, are completely protected by their uncanny resemblance to lichen on lichen-covered bark.

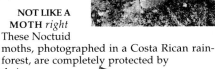

DISAPPEARING CATERPILLAR *left*
By blending with the bark of a tree, this Lappet moth caterpillar (species unknown) is completely protected from predators during daylight hours.

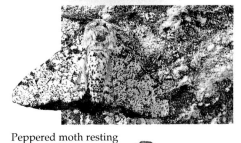

Peppered moth resting on tree in Sherwood Forest, England

DECAYING LEAF *above*
This South American leaf moth, *Belenoptera sanguine,* reproduces a "dead-leaf" pattern on its wings, including the "skeletonized" part often found on dead leaves. When resting, the moth rolls the front part of its wings to resemble a leaf-stalk.

Clear areas that give impression of torn leaf

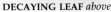

DAMAGED LEAF *above*
To make its leaf-camouflage more realistic, this green Pyralid moth, *Siga liris* (S. America), has irregularly shaped clear areas in its wings. When the moth is resting, these give the impression of a damaged leaf.

Notodontid moth (S. America)

Wood-like camouflage

Notodontid moth (S. America)

WOOD BORER *above*
The caterpillar of this carpenter moth (C. America) bores into trees. As an adult, the moth is almost invisible against bark (right).

Saturniid moth, *Automeris* species, (S. America)

Dead-leaf-like camouflage

VANISHING MOTHS
These three pinned moths have been left with their wings in a normal resting position to show how succesful their camouflage is. In order to survive, they must not look like moths or they would soon be detected by a hungry bird or lizard.

SPOT THE MOTH *above*
It would be impossible to find a better example of how well a moth can blend in with its surroundings than this beautifully patterned but unknown species of carpenter moth.

Mimicry and other unusual behaviour

ALTHOUGH MOST BUTTERFLIES and moths live "normal" lives, there are species that behave unusually. They include moths that can swim underwater, and others whose caterpillars live in ants' nests or beehives. There is also the amazing way in which some species of Lepidoptera mimic other species. If some tropical butterflies seem to advertise themselves with their garish colours and slow flight, it is usually because they are poisonous to predators. But don't be fooled by the "same species" of butterfly flying nearby; it is not poisonous at all, just a very good mimic.

Fruit with hole where adult moth (above right) has pushed its way out after pupation

Caterpillar

JUMPING BEAN MOTH
Jumping Beans, or "vest-pocket pets", are not beans at all but the caterpillar of *Cydia saltitans* (C. America). The "bean" is a small fruit that the caterpillar has bored its way into. When placed near heat, the caterpillar twists and jumps. This may be to move the fruit, with the caterpillar inside, out of direct sunlight.

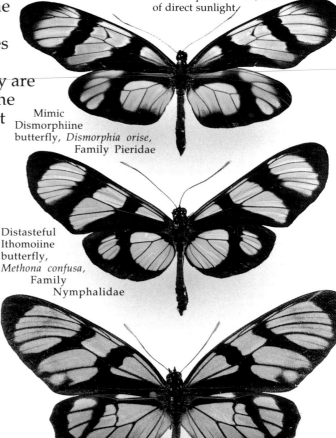

Mimic Dismorphiine butterfly, *Dismorphia orise*, Family Pieridae

Distasteful Ithomoiine butterfly, *Methona confusa*, Family Nymphalidae

Mimic Danaid butterfly, *Lycorea phenarete*, Family Nymphalidae

Mimic Castniid moth, *Gazera linus*, Family Castniidae

SUGAR CANE PEST
The caterpillars of this Galleriid moth, *Eldana saacharina*, are a menace in Africa because they bore into sugar cane stems.

FLOATING MOTH
The caterpillar of this Brown China-mark moth, *Elophila nympheata* (Europe & Asia), lives in waterplants (see opposite page).

DANGEROUS TO CATTLE
This Pyraustine moth, *Filodes sexpunctalis*, is a species of moth that uses its proboscis to feed on the liquid around the eyes of cattle. In doing so it transmits diseases.

AN ENEMY IN THE HIVE
Bee-keepers have to watch out for the caterpillars of the Wax moth, *Galleria* (N. America). The caterpillar not only feeds on the wax but destroys the honeycomb by making silk-lined galleries (right).

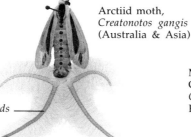

Noctuid moth, (species and place of origin unknown)

Scent tuft has been artificially turned outwards

Arctiid moth, *Creatonotos gangis* (Australia & Asia)

USING THE RIGHT SCENT
The strange-looking tufts protruding from both these moths' abdomens are known as hair-pencils. Evident only in certain species of butterfly and moth, the tufts are a way for the male to disperse his scent and attract a female during courtship.

COPYING YOUR NEIGHBOUR
Although these four South American "butterflies" look amazingly alike, not only do they all belong to different families, but one of them is in fact a moth. The moth and two of the butterflies are protected because the Ithomiine butterfly they mimic is distasteful to predators (more on mimicry on the opposite page).

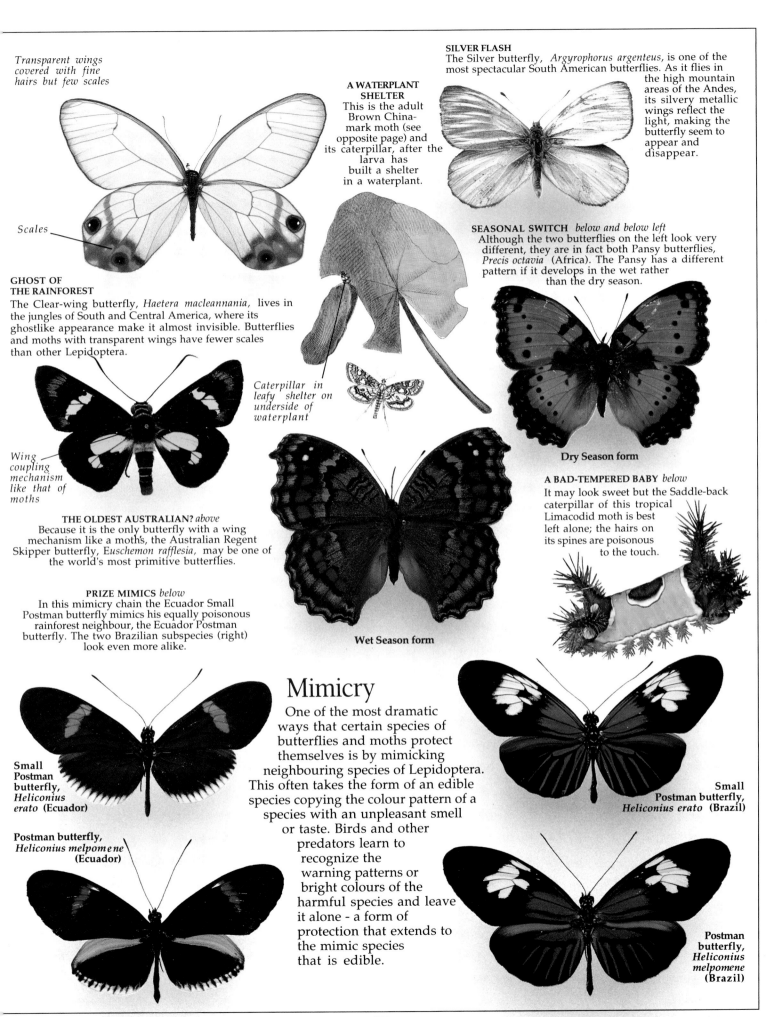

Transparent wings covered with fine hairs but few scales

Scales

SILVER FLASH
The Silver butterfly, *Argyrophorus argenteus*, is one of the most spectacular South American butterflies. As it flies in the high mountain areas of the Andes, its silvery metallic wings reflect the light, making the butterfly seem to appear and disappear.

A WATERPLANT SHELTER
This is the adult Brown China-mark moth (see opposite page) and its caterpillar, after the larva has built a shelter in a waterplant.

GHOST OF THE RAINFOREST
The Clear-wing butterfly, *Haetera macleannania,* lives in the jungles of South and Central America, where its ghostlike appearance make it almost invisible. Butterflies and moths with transparent wings have fewer scales than other Lepidoptera.

Caterpillar in leafy shelter on underside of waterplant

SEASONAL SWITCH *below and below left*
Although the two butterflies on the left look very different, they are in fact both Pansy butterflies, *Precis octavia* (Africa). The Pansy has a different pattern if it develops in the wet rather than the dry season.

Dry Season form

Wing coupling mechanism like that of moths

THE OLDEST AUSTRALIAN? *above*
Because it is the only butterfly with a wing mechanism like a moth's, the Australian Regent Skipper butterfly, *Euschemon rafflesia,* may be one of the world's most primitive butterflies.

A BAD-TEMPERED BABY *below*
It may look sweet but the Saddle-back caterpillar of this tropical Limacodid moth is best left alone; the hairs on its spines are poisonous to the touch.

PRIZE MIMICS *below*
In this mimicry chain the Ecuador Small Postman butterfly mimics his equally poisonous rainforest neighbour, the Ecuador Postman butterfly. The two Brazilian subspecies (right) look even more alike.

Wet Season form

Mimicry

One of the most dramatic ways that certain species of butterflies and moths protect themselves is by mimicking neighbouring species of Lepidoptera. This often takes the form of an edible species copying the colour pattern of a species with an unpleasant smell or taste. Birds and other predators learn to recognize the warning patterns or bright colours of the harmful species and leave it alone - a form of protection that extends to the mimic species that is edible.

Small Postman butterfly, *Heliconius erato* **(Ecuador)**

Postman butterfly, *Heliconius melpomene* **(Ecuador)**

Small Postman butterfly, *Heliconius erato* **(Brazil)**

Postman butterfly, *Heliconius melpomene* **(Brazil)**

57

Endangered species

DEPENDENT AS THEY ARE ON WILD PLANTS and open countryside, butterflies and moths are especially vulnerable to changes in the environment, especially those caused by human beings. In recent times many of these beautiful insects have become first rare, then endangered, then extinct. Butterflies and moths are more common in the tropics than in Europe or North America, but even there the destruction of the rain-forests has reduced their numbers and variety. In milder climates people's need for land has meant that many more insects have become classified as endangered species. Many of these species are listed in the Red Data Book of the International Union for the Conservation of Nature.

BUTTERFLY FRAUD *above*
This famous butterfly fraud dates from about 1702. After painting eyespots on the wings of Brimstone butterflies, the "collector" claimed they were a new species of butterfly, later described as *"Papilio ecclipsis"*.

Painted eyespot

EARLY COLLECTOR *below*
Our knowledge of Lepidoptera is based largely on the work of early collectors such as the Englishman Moses Harris whose classic book *The Aurelian* was published in 1766.

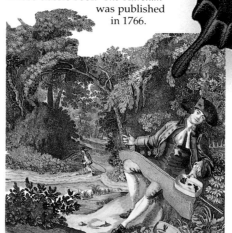

Badly torn wing

Large wings and long tails typical of swallowtails

RECENT DISCOVERY
The Philippines Swallowtail butterfly, *Papilio chikae*, has only recently been discovered. Not only is its habitat threatened, but it is also in danger from keen collectors.

Old engraving of pinned butterfly

LONG-TAILED BEAUTY
Surely the most beautiful European moth, the Spanish Moon Moth, *Graellsia isabellae* (French Alps & Central Spain), now has to be protected by law.

The only European Saturniid moth with tails on its hind wings

Innocent casualties

"As dead as a dodo" is the sad phrase we use for a creature that has become extinct. In the United States the Xerces Blue butterfly has vanished; in Britain several once-common species are now extinct. In Britain enthusiasts have tried to introduce related subspecies from the European mainland to replace the vanished British species. But in other parts of the world extinct species cannot be replaced; and many beautiful insects are now just as dead as the dodo.

The Essex Emerald moth, *Thetidia smaragdaria* (Europe), is now very rare in Britain

Engraving of 19th-century collecting box (left)

Once found in coastal sand dunes of California

IN MEMORY OF
The Xerces Society, a worldwide conservation group, was formed in memory of the Californian Xerces Blue, *Glauscopsyche xerces*, last seen near San Francisco in 1941.

MAKING A COMEBACK *left*
After their habitats were largely destroyed, the Large Copper, and the Large Blue became extinct in Britain. Now, subspecies of both butterflies have been introduced from the European mainland into specially chosen areas of England.

The Large Blue butterfly, *Maculinea arion* (Europe), was recently reintroduced into Southwest England

The beautiful Large Copper butterfly, *Lycaena dispar* (Europe), became extinct in Britain in the 1800s (p. 28)

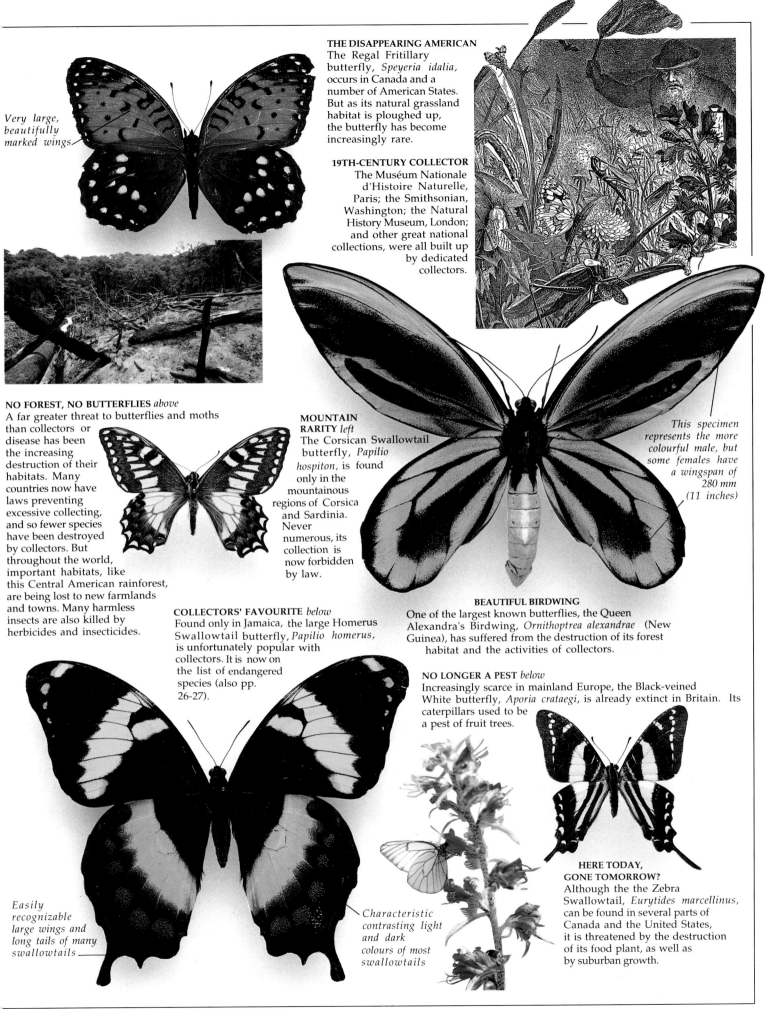

Very large, beautifully marked wings

THE DISAPPEARING AMERICAN
The Regal Fritillary butterfly, *Speyeria idalia*, occurs in Canada and a number of American States. But as its natural grassland habitat is ploughed up, the butterfly has become increasingly rare.

19TH-CENTURY COLLECTOR
The Muséum Nationale d'Histoire Naturelle, Paris; the Smithsonian, Washington; the Natural History Museum, London; and other great national collections, were all built up by dedicated collectors.

NO FOREST, NO BUTTERFLIES *above*
A far greater threat to butterflies and moths than collectors or disease has been the increasing destruction of their habitats. Many countries now have laws preventing excessive collecting, and so fewer species have been destroyed by collectors. But throughout the world, important habitats, like this Central American rainforest, are being lost to new farmlands and towns. Many harmless insects are also killed by herbicides and insecticides.

MOUNTAIN RARITY *left*
The Corsican Swallowtail butterfly, *Papilio hospiton*, is found only in the mountainous regions of Corsica and Sardinia. Never numerous, its collection is now forbidden by law.

This specimen represents the more colourful male, but some females have a wingspan of 280 mm (11 inches)

COLLECTORS' FAVOURITE *below*
Found only in Jamaica, the large Homerus Swallowtail butterfly, *Papilio homerus*, is unfortunately popular with collectors. It is now on the list of endangered species (also pp. 26-27).

BEAUTIFUL BIRDWING
One of the largest known butterflies, the Queen Alexandra's Birdwing, *Ornithoptrea alexandrae* (New Guinea), has suffered from the destruction of its forest habitat and the activities of collectors.

NO LONGER A PEST *below*
Increasingly scarce in mainland Europe, the Black-veined White butterfly, *Aporia crataegi*, is already extinct in Britain. Its caterpillars used to be a pest of fruit trees.

Easily recognizable large wings and long tails of many swallowtails

Characteristic contrasting light and dark colours of most swallowtails

HERE TODAY, GONE TOMORROW?
Although the the Zebra Swallowtail, *Eurytides marcellinus*, can be found in several parts of Canada and the United States, it is threatened by the destruction of its food plant, as well as by suburban growth.

Watching butterflies and moths

FOR MANY YEARS people have collected butterflies and moths as a hobby and for scientific study. But it is better for the insects themselves, as well as more interesting and rewarding, to watch them in the field. You can also photograph butterflies, or catch them in a net for closer examination before releasing them again. Most moths fly at night, but it is possible to study members of day-flying families. When watching butterflies and moths, you can discover the answers to many questions about their behaviour. Do they feed at a certain time of day? Do they have a territory, and if so, how do they defend it? Do they migrate, and if so, when? Do their flight patterns change in different seasons? Studying butterflies in this way is simple: you do not require much apparatus, and you need not harm them - all you need is patience.

A 19th-century interpretation of the fashion for insect collecting

PINNING THEM DOWN
Compiling a butterfly collection was once a popular pastime.

WARNING FOR COLLECTORS
Many butterflies are protected by law, and in some countries collecting without a permit is forbidden. In Britain, a permit is required for the study of certain rare species. Collecting and study on nature reserves is usually also carefully controlled. A number of butterflies cannot be collected and sent out of the country without a permit. International conventions regulate trade in endangered species. Always check the local regulations.

WRITING AND RECORDING
Use a notebook (above) or tape recorder (below) to make notes on each butterfly's appearance and behaviour, together with the date, time, weather conditions, and details of the locality. A good field guide helps in identification.

Macro lens (that enlarges images) for close-ups

CLOSE-UP CAMERA
An SLR camera with a macro lens is ideal. Bright sunlight will give the best results; use flash in the shade.

SHORT-FOCUS TELESCOPE
In the field, use an 8 x 20 short-focus optical telescope (which has a magnification of x 8 and a lens diameter of 20 mm).

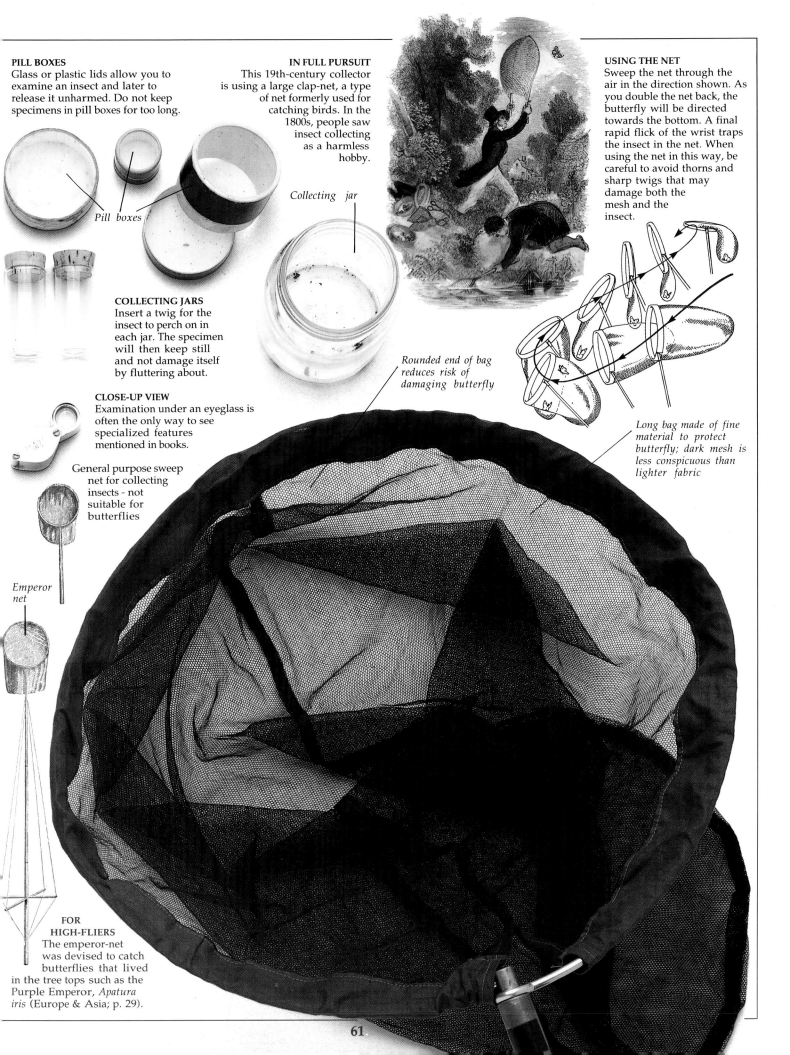

PILL BOXES
Glass or plastic lids allow you to examine an insect and later to release it unharmed. Do not keep specimens in pill boxes for too long.

Pill boxes

IN FULL PURSUIT
This 19th-century collector is using a large clap-net, a type of net formerly used for catching birds. In the 1800s, people saw insect collecting as a harmless hobby.

Collecting jar

USING THE NET
Sweep the net through the air in the direction shown. As you double the net back, the butterfly will be directed towards the bottom. A final rapid flick of the wrist traps the insect in the net. When using the net in this way, be careful to avoid thorns and sharp twigs that may damage both the mesh and the insect.

COLLECTING JARS
Insert a twig for the insect to perch on in each jar. The specimen will then keep still and not damage itself by fluttering about.

Rounded end of bag reduces risk of damaging butterfly

Long bag made of fine material to protect butterfly; dark mesh is less conspicuous than lighter fabric

CLOSE-UP VIEW
Examination under an eyeglass is often the only way to see specialized features mentioned in books.

General purpose sweep net for collecting insects - not suitable for butterflies

Emperor net

FOR HIGH-FLIERS
The emperor-net was devised to catch butterflies that lived in the tree tops such as the Purple Emperor, *Apatura iris* (Europe & Asia; p. 29).

Index

Acknowledgments

Dorling Kindersley would like to thank:
The staff at the London Butterfly House; also Tom Fox for his advice, and David Lees for his advice and for providing butterfly eggs and caterpillars.
The staff at the British Museum (Natural History), in particular Mr. P. Ackery, Mr D. Carter, Miss J. Goode, Mr C. Owen, Mr. C. Smith and Mr A. Watson. Colin Mays of Worldwide Butterflies for providing the silkworms on pp. 40-41.
Stephen Bull, and Fred Ford and Mike Pilley of Radius Graphics for artwork.

Picture credits
t=top b=bottom m=middle l=left r=right c=centre

Ardea London: 26br; 27br; 35tc; 37mr; 50ml; 51mr, br; 52mr; 55ml, bl; 57mr
The Bridgeman Art Library: 6tl; 24t
The Trustees of the British Museum: 6br
The British Museum (Natural History): 58t, mc
Professor Frank Carpenter: 6bl
E.T. Archives: 12t; 49mr
Fine Art Photographs: 63br
Heather Angel: 26bl; 27bl
Jeremy Thomas/Biofotos: 31tr
John Freeman London: 34ml; 45tr
Mansell Collection: 14t; 40tl, bl
Mary Evans Picture Library: 10t; 40tr; 56tl; 60tl

Oxford Scientific Films Ltd: 11bl; 45mr; 55tc, mr; 56mc; 59tl
Paul Whalley: 29tc; 38ml; 59bc; 61tr
Quadrant Picture Library: 44ml
Royal Botanic Gardens, Kew: 33mc
Sonia Halliday Photographs: 40m

Illustrations by: Coral Mula for pp. 61, 62-63; Sandra Pond for pp 50-51; Christine Robins for pp. 16-17, 18-19, 28-29, 30, 32.

Picture research by: Millie Trowbridge.